CW00587842

GUN LAW
IN ENGLAND AND WALES

GUN LAW

By

Godfrey Sandys-Winsch, B.A. (Cantab.)
Solicitor

FIFTH EDITION

London:
Published by
SHAW & SONS LTD.
Shaway House, SE26 5AE
1990

First Published	...	...	...	...	...	...	February 1969
Second Edition	...	...	...	...	...	...	... April 1973
Third Edition	...	...	...	...	...	...	February 1979
Fourth Edition	...	...	...	...	...	...	April 1985
Fifth Edition	...	...	...	...	...	...	... April 1990

British Library Cataloguing in Publication Data
Sandys-Winsch, Godfrey
  Gun law.—5th ed.
  1. England. Firearms. Law
  I. Title
  344.204533

  ISBN 0–7219–0363–0

© SHAW & SONS LTD. 1990
Printed in Great Britain

CONTENTS

[v]

APPENDICES

PREFACE TO FIFTH EDITION

This Edition has been prompted by the enactment on 15th November 1988 of the Firearms (Amendment) 1988, the first major reform of firearms law for 20 years. That Act, in turn, was the result of the Hungerford incident on 19th August 1987, the Government being finally persuaded thereby that tighter controls over especially lethal kinds of weapons were called for.

In summary, the main effect of the 1988 Act is to classify as prohibited weapons self-loading and pump-action rifles and short barrelled smooth bore guns, "burst fire" weapons and rocket launchers and mortars. Other measures in the Act include the tightening of controls on ordinary shot guns.

The provisions of the new Act were brought into force in stages by means of two commencement orders which, subject to some transitional provisions, had the result of making the whole Act effective by 1st October, 1989.

The foregoing alterations in firearms law have suggested to me that most of it would be better presented in a different format. I have therefore written individual chapters on prohibited weapons, Section 1 firearms, shot guns and air weapons; each chapter deals with all aspects of the law affecting the particular type of gun, though that relating to young persons has remained in a separate chapter. Separate chapters have also been written on police permits, visitors' permits and the new museum firearms licences.

Other changes in statutory law have been mimimal. Decisions on a few court cases published since the last Edition have been added.

I wish to thank Mr. P.J. Goulder of the Home Office for his help with some aspects of the new law.

GODFREY SANDYS-WINSCH

LEASINGHAM,
LINCOLNSHIRE.   *January 1990.*

PREFACE TO FIRST EDITION

I have ventured to write this small book on a subject which, to the best of my belief, has not before had devoted to it a separate book. It seemed to me that there might be a wide need for such a book, from a father wondering whether he could allow his son to use an air gun to the police and others in authority who might not have the answers at their fingertips.

It was my intention, when I began writing, to produce a book in simple terms and primarily for the ordinary person who handles a gun. Alas, it soon became apparent that the complications of the law would not allow the attainment of the first object. I have, nevertheless, tried to keep the text as straightforward as possible, but am conscious that in so doing I may have fallen between the virtue of simplicity on the one hand and the need for comprehensiveness on the other.

The law governing the use of guns is sometimes a strange mixture of the old and the new: there is the body of legislation passed between 1825 and 1850 and retained in the verbiage of an age when the infringement of gaming rights was so seriously regarded that a poacher might be transported overseas for 14 years; modern society has, on the other hand, been more concerned to curb the indiscriminate and illegal use of guns by its less responsible members and to protect wild life. This is not to say that poaching is no longer a problem; in many rural areas it is still prevalent, though the modern poacher is often, by background and method of operation, a very different fellow from his predecessor of 100 years ago.

The law relating to guns has been subjected to recent change as much as any other branch of the law, and this has necessarily added to the difficulties of writing. Gun licences were abolished on 13th December 1966, and shot gun certificates were introduced on 1st May 1968.

The law is stated in the book as at 1st January 1969.

Because, as I have said, this book was intended primarily

for the ordinary person who handles a gun, I have not dealt with the following matters: military weapons; what may be called "vicious offences", by which I mean the use of guns by the criminal classes; the regulations affecting game dealers; the killing of birds and animals otherwise than by shooting, except occasionally for purposes of completing a passage in the text; and the law outside England and Wales.

I readily acknowledge the help which I have received, particularly on some of the more difficult points concerning game, from Oke's Game Laws, the last edition of which was published in 1912 and which I believe to be the only book extant (but not readily available) on the subject.

In conclusion, I would like to express my gratitude to the Home Office for the ready and comprehensive advice given on certain topics, and to Superintendent E. Beverley and Mr. A. M. Duffin for their most valuable help in perusing parts of the manuscript.

GODFREY SANDYS-WINSCH

LEASINGHAM,
LINCOLNSHIRE.   *January 1969.*

TABLE OF STATUTES

[xiii]

TABLE OF CASES

[xxi]

CHAPTER 1

FIREARMS AND AMMUNITION: DEFINITIONS AND GENERAL EXCEPTIONS

Introduction

The main body of the criminal law regulating the use of firearms and ammunition is contained in the Firearms Acts of 1968 and 1982 as now amended by the Firearms (Amendment) Act of 1988. Such parts of that law as are covered in this book are dealt with in Chapters 2 to 9, 14, 15 (part) and 16, where the words "firearm" and "ammunition" frequently appear. Whilst, as will be seen, the meanings of these words are very wide and will cover all ordinary cases, it is appropriate, by way of this introductory Chapter, to examine their precise meanings. For certain purposes particular kinds of weapons are given their own definitions; this is so in the case of prohibited weapons, Section 1 firearms, shot guns and slaughtering instruments. These definitions are dealt with in later Chapters as and when they occur.

The operation of this code of criminal law in the three Firearms Acts is totally excluded in two cases which are, briefly, the proving of firearms and the handling of antique weapons. It seems appropriate also to deal with these two matters in this opening Chapter.

Definition of "Firearm"

The word "firearm" is lengthily defined in the 1968 Act, and several ingredients of this definition must be examined with a number of interpretative decisions of the Courts. The definition readily falls into two parts: the core of the definition, and the particular additions to it.

I THE CORE OF THE DEFINITION

This reads: the expression "firearm" means a lethal barrelled weapon of any description from which any shot, bullet or other missile can be discharged.[1] The following words in this part of the definition require individual examination:

(a) *Lethal*

> By dictionary definition this means: causing, sufficient or designed to cause, death. In fact a weapon does not have to be as deadly as this definition might at first sight suggest, as is shown by the following two cases:

Case (A) This was a double-barrelled signal pistol with a small propelling charge firing a cartridge with explosive ballistite and containing a phosphorus and magnesium flare. It was capable of killing at short range and might be fatal up to 20 feet. Therefore it was lethal, and the intentions of the designer or manufacturer of the weapon were immaterial.[2]

Case (B) The least powerful type of air gun, which normally would cause only trivial injury, can nevertheless be classed as lethal because its pellet, fired at a particularly vulnerable point such as an eye, could cause death.[3]

---

[1] F.A. 1968 s. 57 (1).
[2] *Read v. Donovan* [1947] 1 All E.R. 37.
[3] *Moore v. Gooderham* [1960] 3 All E.R. 575; *R. v. Thorpe* [1987] 2 All E.R. 108..

(b) Barrelled

The relevant dictionary definition of "barrel" is: cylindrical body or trunk of an object; metal tube of gun. Thus, a barrel must at least be cylindrical; it would not be sufficient for the missile to be discharged along a groove or channel which was unenclosed for any part of its circumference. Despite the second part of the definition, it is suggested that the barrel may be made of any substance.

The length of the barrel is immaterial in this context.[1]

(c) Weapon

The dictionary defines a "weapon" as a material thing designed or used or usable as an instrument for inflicting bodily harm.[2]

(d) Any shot, bullet or other missile

Following the general rule for construing Acts of Parliament, the meaning of the words "or other missile" must be confined to things of the same kind as shot and bullet. This leads to the probable conclusion that the missile must be a solid object; thus a dart from an air gun would be included, but not liquid or gas.[3]

(e) Can be discharged

Here, also, the normal meaning of these words has been expanded by decisions of the Courts. The fact that a gun at the time of an offence is not capable of discharging a missile will not necessarily prevent it from fulfilling this part of the definition, as is shown by the following three cases:

---

[1] It is, however, material in the definition of a shot gun, as to which *see* p. 41.

[2] An electric stunning device is a weapon (*Flack v. Baldry* [1988] 1 All E.R. 673).

[3] In the absence of any Court decision on the point, this interpretation can be tentative only. For guns and ammunition discharging a noxious liquid, gas or other thing, *see* pp. 12–14.

4 FIREARMS AND AMMUNITION

Case (A) This was a dummy revolver, with the shape and appearance of an ordinary revolver, with a barrel which was solid except for a hole which was drilled in 3/8ths of an inch from the muzzle. The revolving "cartridge chamber" was also solid except for shallow recesses at the ends of what would ordinarily be the cartridge chambers, and there was a venthole for the escape of gas. In that state it was not capable of firing a bullet or other missile, but by five minutes electric drilling the necessary parts could be made to do so sufficiently to kill a man at five feet.

the definition of "firearm" in that case described it as "any lethal firearm or other weapon of any description from which any shot, bullet, or other missile can be discharged, or any part thereof".

HELD: the dummy revolver was a firearm within that definition because: it contained everything else necessary for making a revolver except the barrel and therefore all the other parts of it, except those which required to be bored, were "parts thereof" within the quoted definition; or, alternatively, the dummy as a whole was part of a firearm within the definition and, by adding something to it or adapting it, the dummy would be a complete revolver.[1]

Case (B) This was a Scottish case concerning a double-barrelled pistol the barrels of which had been pierced but if the holes had been blocked up the pistol would have been capable of firing live ammunition. The Court decided that the pistol was a firearm.[2]

---

[1] *Cafferata v. Wilson* [1936] 3 All E.R. 149. In the Scottish case of *Kelly v. MacKinnon* (1983 S.L.T. 9) a replica revolver capable of being converted to fire live ammunition was held to be a firearm.
[2] *Muir v. Cassidy* 1953 S.L.T. (Sh. Ct.) 4.

Case (c) This was a .38 starting pistol with a revolving chamber and of solid construction. The firing chambers had constrictions at the front ends. The barrel was solid except that at the muzzle end a hole had been drilled coming out at the top behind the front sight. By drilling the necessary parts the gun could fire bullets with lethal force. HELD: following Case (A) above, the pistol was a firearm within the definition.[1]

The Firearms (Amendment) Act 1988 has intervened in this field by providing that a firearm shall be presumed, unless the contrary is shown, to be incapable of discharging any shot, bullet or other missile and has consequently ceased to be a firearm within the definition of that word, if—

(a) it bears an approved[2] mark denoting that fact which has been made *either* by:
　(i) the Worshipful Company of Gunmakers of London or the Guardians of the Birmingham proof house; *or*
　(ii) some other approved[2] person, *and*
(b) the company or person making the mark has certified in writing that the work has been done in a manner approved[2] for rendering the firearm incapable of discharge[3].

Before leaving this part of the definition it should be noted that there is no limitation on the means of propulsion of the missile. The explosive charge is most common, and compressed air is used for air weapons, but the use of other

---

[1] *R. v. Freeman* [1970] 2 All E.R. 413. Although the effect of this decision is as stated, the main argument in the case was directed to the point as to whether the interpretation of the similar definition of "firearm" in the Firearms Act 1920 was still applicable.

In the Scottish case of *Kelly v. MacKinnon* (1983 S.L.T. 9) a starting pistol capable of being converted to fire live ammunition was held to be a firearm.

[2] *I.e.*, approved by the Secretary of State for the Home Office. The approved marks and the approved manner of work may be found in "Firearms Law: Specifications for the Adaptation of Shot Gun Magazines and the De-activation of Firearms" obtainable from H.M.S.O. bookshops.

[3] F.A. 1968 s. 58(1); F.(A)A. 1988 s. 8.

forces, *e.g.* springs, elastic or tension as used in a bow, is acceptable.

What are the more important points which emerge from this examination of this part of the definition?

The meaning of the word "lethal" has been widened; the cheapest kind of air gun would not ordinarily be described as a deadly weapon. A weapon can be lethal even if it can cause mortal injury only by striking at a specially vulnerable point; and it matters not, it seems, if this can be achieved only by using the weapon at point-blank range. The fact that the weapon was never designed or sold for killing, or even harming, any person or thing is irrelevant.

On the question of discharge, and leaving aside the new procedure under the 1988 Act as described above, cases (A), (B) and (C) have decided that, at the material time, a weapon need not be capable of discharging a missile. It appears that it is enough if it can be made to do so by work on it, or adaptations to it, which can easily and quickly be done; five minutes' work with an electric drill was cited in Case (A). The questions "How easily?" and "How quickly?" are thus unsatisfactorily left open for each case to be decided on its particular facts but with the precedents of these three cases for guidance.[1]

II THE PARTICULAR ADDITIONS TO THE DEFINITION

After the core of the definition, which has just been discussed, the Act goes on to say—

"and includes—

(*a*) any prohibited weapon, whether it is such a lethal weapon as aforesaid or not; and

(*b*) any component part of such a lethal or prohibited weapon; and

(*c*) any accessory to any such weapon designed or

---

[1] As to conversion of an imitation firearm so as to bring it within the definition of "firearm" here discussed, see pp. 62–63.

adapted to diminish the noise or flash caused by firing the weapon."[1]

Certain words in this part of the definition also need individual examination.

(1) *Prohibited Weapon*

The meaning of "prohibited weapon" is discussed at length in Chapter 2.

(2) *Component Parts and Accessories*

It is clear from a reading of paragraphs (*b*) and (*c*) of this part of the definition that a component part or accessory is not caught by the definition unless the weapon to which it is related is itself a firearm within the definition discussed above or a prohibited weapon as described in Chapter 2.

There is one reported decision of the Courts about component parts and accessories:

> W. possessed a .22 rifle with a removable telescopic sight which was not an original part of the rifle as manufactured but had been made by W. The rifle was designed to be and could be used without the sight. W.'s firearm certificate mentioned the rifle and a silencer but not the sight. He was prosecuted for possessing the sight as a component part of a firearm without being authorised to do so by a firearm certificate, it being argued that the sight should have been referred to in the certificate. The Court's decision was that W.'s certificate covered his possession of the sight although it was a component part of the rifle.[2]

The following conclusions can be drawn from this decision and the wording of the definition:–

> (i) The term "component part" will include, as well as an essential part of a gun such as the trigger, other parts not indispensable to its use

---

[1] F.A. 1968 s. 57 (1).
[2] *Watson v. Herman* [1952] 2 All E.R. 70.

B

and which would ordinarily be regarded as accessories, *e.g.* a telescopic sight.

(ii) An accessory for diminishing noise or flash and used with a gun must be covered by a firearm certificate, *i.e.* be mentioned in a certificate as well as the gun to which it is related.

(iii) A firearm certificate specifying a particular weapon will, without mentioning them, cover all parts of that weapon and all its accessories unless of the kind described in (ii).

(iv) Component parts and accessories of the kind described in (ii) when held by themselves require the possession of a firearm certificate.

Definition of "Ammunition"

The definition in the Firearms Act 1968 says that "ammunition" means: ammunition for any firearm and includes grenades, bombs and other missiles, whether capable of use with a firearm or not, and also includes prohibited ammunition.[1] There are three points in this which require examination.

(a) Ammunition for any firearm

The use of the words "any firearm" indicates that the definition includes ammunition for a firearm which does not fall within the definition of "firearm" as earlier discussed; in other words, the definition of "firearm" does not apply in this context.[2]

(b) Parts of ammunition

Unlike the definition of "firearm", there is no reference to a component part, and therefore the ingredients or com-

---

[1] F.A. 1968 s. 57 (2).

[2] This view is reinforced by the fact that in the earlier Firearms Act of 1937 the wording of the first part of the definition was: ammunition for any firearm *as hereinafter defined*. The inference is therefore that in the 1968 Act the definition of "firearm" does not apply.

ponent parts of a piece of ammunition are not caught by the definition.

(c) Prohibited Ammunition

The meaning of "prohibited ammunition" is discussed at length in Chapter 2.

General Exceptions

The first exception arises in the case of proving firearms. The Firearms Act 1968 says:

"Nothing in this Act shall apply to the proof houses of the Master, Wardens and Society of the Mystery of Gunmakers of the City of London and the guardians of the Birmingham proof house or the rifle range at Small Heath in Birmingham where firearms are sighted and tested, so as to interfere in any way with the operations of those two companies in proving firearms under the provisions of the Gun Barrel Proof Act 1868 or any other Acts for the time bring in force, or to any person carrying firearms to or from any such proof house when being taken to such proof house for the purposes of proof or being removed therefrom after proof."[1]

The second exception deals with antique firearms. The provisions of the Act do not apply to an antique firearm which is sold, transferred,[2] purchased, acquired[3] or possessed[4] as a curiosity or ornament.[5]

The first point to be considered here is: when is a firearm an antique? The Act itself does not assist in any way. Until 1977 there was some support for the proposition that a firearm only became an antique when it was 100 years old.

---

[1] F.A. 1968 s. 57 (1).
[2] This word is defined to *include* let on hire, given, lent, and parted with possession (F.A. 1968 s. 57 (4)).
[3] This word is defined to mean hired, accepted as a gift or borrowed (F.A. 1968 s. 57 (4)).
[4] For commentary on the meaning of "possessed", see pp. 20–22.
[5] F.A. 1968 S.58(2).

A decision of the High Court in that year[1] rejected that approach holding that the question of whether a firearm was an antique or not was a question of fact and degree to be left to the good sense and judgement of the magistrates trying each case. It was wrong, the Court said, to fix a particular age at which a firearm should be said to become an antique. The Court indicated that factors which might properly be taken into account in deciding whether a firearm is an antique or not are: whether the owner is a genuine collector of old firearms; whether he possesses them as curiosities or ornaments; and whether they have peculiar value because of their age.

This decision would have helped to some extent if its criteria had not been upset by a 1980 case which laid down that a firearm manufactured in this century could not be an antique.[2] However, the latest Home Office guidance to the police, taking a more lenient view, indicates that some categories of firearms manufactured up to the Second World War may be classified as antiques.[3]

The second point to note is that antique firearms are only excluded from the operation of the 1968 Act when possessed or handled **as a curiosity or ornament**. Using them in any other way, for example by firing them, removes this protection.

A second court case in 1977[4] dealt with the situation where a defendant had bought a modern reproduction of a type of revolver manufactured over 100 years ago believing it to be a genuine antique and pleading that as a defence. This was not accepted, the Court holding that only the true facts of the situation, not beliefs, were relevant, even if those beliefs were honestly and reasonably held.

---

[1] *Richards v. Curwen* [1977] 3 All E.R. 426. The case concerned revolvers 83 and 85 years old respectively.

[2] *Bennett v. Brown* [1980] Cr. App. R. 109, when an 1886 weapon was accepted as an antique but two others made after 1905 and 1910 respectively were not.

[3] *"Firearms Law: Guidance to the Police"* 1989. This guidance in tabular form is reproduced in Appendix A at the end of the book.

[4] *R. v. Howells* [1977] 3 All E.R. 417.

CHAPTER 2

PROHIBITED WEAPONS AND AMMUNITION

Definition of prohibited weapons

The main purpose of the Firearms (Amendment) Act 1988, following the Hungerford incident in August 1987, is to extend the list of prohibited weapons set out in the Firearms Act of 1968.[1] The weapons added to the list are, briefly: self-loading and pump action guns, smooth-bore revolver guns, rocket launchers and mortars. The new definition of prohibited weapon, as expressed in the words of the two Acts,[2] is as follows: —

(*a*) Any firearm which is so designed or adapted that two or more missiles can be successively discharged without repeated pressure on the trigger.

(*b*) Any self-loading[3] or pump-action[4] rifle[5] other than one which is chambered for .22 rim-fire cartridges.

(*c*) Any self-loading[3] or pump-action[4] smooth-bore gun which is not chambered for .22 rim-fire cartridges

---

[1] See s. 5(1) of that Act.

[2] F.A. 1968 s. 5(1)(b); F.(A)A. 1988 s. 1(1), (2).

[3] This means a weapon designed or adapted, except as in (*a*) above, so that it is automatically re-loaded. (F.A. 1968 s. 57(2A); F.(A)A. 1988 s. 25(2)).

[4] This means a weapon so designed or adapted, except as in (*a*) above, that it is re-loaded by the manual operation of its fore-end or forestock. (F.A. 1968 s. 57(2A); F.(A)A. 1988 s. 25(2)).

[5] "Rifle" includes carbine. (F.A. 1968 s. 57(4); F.(A)A. 1988 s. 25(3)). There is no reason to suppose that the term will exclude an air rifle.

and either has a barrel less than 24 inches long[1] **or** (excluding any detachable, folding, retractable or other movable butt-stock) is less than 40 inches long overall.

(d) Any smooth-bore revolver gun[2] other than one which is chambered for 9 mm. rim-fire cartridges or loaded at the muzzle end of each chamber.[3]

(e) Any rocket launcher, or any mortar, for projecting a stabilised missile, other than a launcher or mortar designed for line-throwing[4] or pyrotechnic purposes[5] or as signalling apparatus.[6]

(f) Any weapon of whatever description designed or adapted for the discharge of any noxious liquid, gas or other thing.

As to (f) above, the words "weapon of whatever description" show that the weapon need not be any sort of gun or in any way resemble a gun.[7] A dictionary definition of a weapon is: a material thing designed or used or usable as an instrument for inflicting bodily harm.

The word "noxious", meaning harmful or unwholesome, is thought to apply to the words "gas" and "other thing" as well as to "liquid". The words "other thing" should be interpreted, it is suggested, as meaning "any other thing of any kind"; i.e., their meaning is not restricted to a thing which is of the same kind as liquid or gas.[8] Thus, it appears that the last seven words in item (f) could be written as

---

[1] The measurement is from the muzzle to the point at which the charge is exploded on firing (F.A. 1968 s. 57(6)(a); F.(A)A. 1988 s. 25(1)).

[2] This means a gun containing a series of chambers which revolve when the gun is fired. (F.A. 1968 s. 57(2B); F.(A)A. 1988 s. 25(2)).

[3] A smooth-bore revolver gun which is so chambered or so loaded will be classified as a Section 1 firearm, for which see Chapter 3.

[4] E.g., for coastguard rescue purposes.

[5] I.e., for firework displays.

[6] E.g., for firing flares.

[7] This is demonstrated by the case at note 1 on p. 13.

[8] This construction is different from that applied to the words "any shot, bullet or other missile" on p. 3 because the words "liquid" and "gas" do not constitute a category or class of thing. (*Halsbury's Laws of England*, 4th Edition, Vol. 44, para. 87).

"any noxious liquid, any noxious gas, or any noxious thing[1] of any kind".[2]

The Home Office may by order add firearms of other descriptions to the foregoing list.[3]

A weapon which—

(i) has at any time been a weapon of a kind described in items (a) to (f) above, **and**
(ii) is not a self-loading[4] or pump action[5] smooth-bore gun which has at any time been a weapon of the type described at (i) above by reason only of having had a barrel less than 24 inches long[6]—

is to be treated as a prohibited weapon notwithstanding anything done to convert it into a different kind of weapon.[7]

There are three court decisions concerned with automatic weapons which had been modified or adapted or were incomplete. It has been held that a sub-machine gun which had been modified to prevent it from being fired when the automatic mode was selected was not a prohibited weapon.[8] But an adaption to the trigger mechanism of an automatic weapon making the firing of single shots easier did not prevent the weapon from being an automatic weapon and therefore prohibited.[9] The third case concerned a sub-machine gun lacking three parts which could easily be

---

[1] Electricity is a noxious thing and its discharge by means of an electric stunning device is a discharge within the meaning of that word in item (f) above. Such a device is therefore a prohibited weapon (*Flack v. Baldry* [1988] 1 All ER 673). Likewise, weapons specially designed or adapted to discharge tranquillising darts are prohibited weapons. Cattle prods are not.

[2] In the absence of any Court decisions on the point, this interpretation can be tentative only.

[3] F.(A)A. 1988 s. 1(4).

[4] For the meaning of "self-loading", see note 3 on p. 11.

[5] For the meaning of "pump action", see note 4 on p. 11.

[6] For the measurement of this length, see note 1 on p. 12.

[7] F.(A)A. 1988 s. 7(1).

[8] *R. v. Jobling* [1981] Crim. LR 625.

[9] *R. v. Pannell* (1983) 76 Crim. App. R. 53, CA.

replaced so as to make it fire normally; the Court decided that the gun was a prohibited weapon.[1]

These decisions must now be interpreted in the light of the statutory provisions above about converted weapons. It would appear that those provisions would apply in the circumstances of the first and second cases but not in those of the third.

Definition of Prohibited Ammunition

As in the case of prohibited weapons, the definition of prohibited ammunition has been much widened by the Firearms (Amendment) Act of 1988. The definition now reads as follows:

(1) Any cartridge with a bullet designed to explode on or immediately before impact.[2]
(2) Any ammunition containing, or designed or adapted to contain, any such noxious thing as is mentioned at item (f) on page 12.[3]
(3) If capable of being used with a firearm of any description,[4] any grenade, bomb (or other like missile), or rocket or shell designed to explode as in (1) above.[5]

The Home Office may by order add ammunition of other descriptions to the foregoing list.[6]

Dealings with Prohibited Weapons and Ammunition

Owing to the nature of prohibited weapons and ammunition, there are only limited circumstances in which you

---

[1] *R. v. Clarke (Frederick)* [1986] 1 All ER 846. The Court also decided that, in any case, the incomplete gun constituted component parts of a prohibited weapon which fell within the definition of that kind of weapon by virtue of F.A. 1968 s. 57(1)(b). See pp. 7–8.

[2] Tracer bullets and hollow-point and soft-point bullets are not within this definition.

[3] A tranquillising dart is thus prohibited ammunition. For commentary on "noxious things", see that page and the notes thereto.

[4] *I.e.*, including a firearm which does not fall within the definition of that term as discussed in Chapter 1.

[5] F.A. 1968 s. 5(1)(c), (2); F.(A)A. 1988 s. 1(3).

[6] F.(A)A. 1988 s. 1(4).

will be entitled to handle them lawfully. With the exceptions mentioned below, you will commit an offence[1] if you have in your possession,[2] purchase, acquire,[3] manufacture, sell or transfer[4] any prohibited weapon or prohibited ammunition. The exceptions are: —

(a) When you have the special authority of the Home Office.[5] This is only issued after careful enquiries by the police and seldom to a private individual.

(b) When your handling of the weapons or ammunition is covered by a museum firearms licence.[6]

(c) When a special authority from the Home Office is held for acting purposes. If the Home Office is satisfied that a prohibited weapon is required for a theatrical performance, a rehearsal thereof or the production of a film, they may authorise the person in charge to have possession[7] of the weapon. That authority may also include possession[7] by others selected by that person while they are taking part in the performance, rehearsal or production.[8]

The widened descriptions of prohibited weapons detailed on pages 11 and 12 became effective on 1st February 1989. However, if, immediately before that date, you lawfully possessed a firearm which thereafter became a prohibited weapon, you were entitled to continue to possess it and sell or otherwise transfer[9] it up to and including 30th April 1989.

---

[1] The maximum punishment on summary conviction is imprisonment for 6 months, or the statutory maximum fine (currently £2000), or both; or, on indictment, 5 years' imprisonment, or an unlimited fine, or both. (F.A. 1968 ss. 5(1), 51(1)(2) and Schedule 6, Part I).

[2] For some guidance on the meaning of "possession", see pp. 20–22.

[3] This word is defined to mean hire, accept as a gift or borrow. (F.A. 1968 s. 57(4)).

[4] This word is defined to include let on hire, give, lend and part with possession. (F.A. 1968 s. 57(4)).

[5] F.A. 1968 s. 5(1). Further provisions about the special authority are in F.A. 1968 s. 5(3)–(6). Applications for an authority should be made to the Home Office (F8 Division), 50 Queen Anne's Gate, London SW1H 9AT.

[6] For this kind of licence, see Chapter 8.

[7] Note that possession only is covered.

[8] F.A. 1968 ss. 5, 12(2); F.(A)A. 1988 s. 23(2).

[9] "Transfer" includes give, lend and part with possession (F.A. 1968 s. 57(4); the Commencement Order cited at note 4 on p. 16, Article 4(2)).

In the case of a registered firearms dealer,[1] the entitlement extended to the possession, purchase, acquisition,[2] sale and transfer[3] of such a firearm with a terminal date of 31st October 1989.[4]

The holding of a special authority given by the Home Office for a prohibited weapon or ammunition does not obviate the need for a firearm certificate, but the police are not entitled to refuse to grant or renew, or to revoke, a firearm certificate whilst the special authority is in force.[5]

Compensation for Surrendered Weapons

As we have seen on pages 11 and 12, the descriptions of weapons now classified as prohibited have been widened by the Firearms (Amendment) Act of 1988. There are thus some weapons which formerly could be lawfully held if covered by the appropriate firearm or shot gun certificate but which, when the new legislation became effective, could not be so held unless specially authorised as just described.

To meet this situation, the Home Office are to make a scheme providing for payments to persons who surrender or otherwise dispose of firearms which they can no longer hold under certificates. To qualify for compensation,[6]—

(1) The person must have possessed[7] the firearm immediately before 23rd September 1987;[8] **and**
(2) That possession at that time must have been covered by the appropriate certificate.

---

[1] As to the registration of firearms dealers, see pp. 137–140.

[2] "Acquisition" means hiring, accepting as a gift or borrowing (F.A. 1968 s. 57(4)).

[3] For the meaning of "transfer", see note 9 on p. 15.

[4] Firearms (Amendment) Act 1988 (Commencement No. 1) Order 1988. The above provisions extend to a converted firearm which is to be treated as a prohibited weapon, for which see p. 13.

[5] F.A. 1968 ss. 1(1), (3), (4), 31(1).

[6] The scheme, yet to be made, may itself contain other conditions.

[7] For some guidance on the meaning of "possessed", see pp. 20–22.

[8] This date is the day following that on which the Home Secretary first announced the Government's intention to prohibit certain specially dangerous types of firearms.

If there was a contract to acquire[1] a firearm before 23rd September 1987[2] and possession on or after that date was covered by the appropriate certificate, compensation is also payable.[3]

---

[1] This word is defined to mean hire, accept as a gift or borrow, (F.A. 1968 s. 57(4); F.(A)A. 1988 s. 25(1)).

[2] As to this date, see note 8 on p. 16.

[3] F.(A)A. 1988 s. 21.

CHAPTER 3

SECTION ONE FIREARMS AND AMMUNITION

Definition of Section 1 Firearm

The term "Section 1 firearms" is commonly applied to those guns which are caught by the definition in Section 1 of the Firearms Act 1968 and which, in general, require a firearm certificate for lawful use.

These firearms are mainly defined by exception,[1] but include one type of gun which can be positively identified. Rules made by the Home Office[2] have declared the more powerful kinds of air weapons to be specially dangerous. These are an air rifle or an air gun capable of discharging a missile so that the missile has, on discharge from the muzzle, kinetic energy exceeding 12 ft. lb.; in the case of an air pistol, the kinetic energy figure is 6 ft. lb. But the declaration does not apply to an air weapon designed for use only when submerged in water.

In total, Section 1 firearms consist of—

(A) Specially dangerous air weapons; and

---

[1] F.A. 1968 s. 1(3).
[2] The Firearms (Dangerous Air Weapons) Rules 1969 made under the authority of F.A. 1968 ss. 1(3)(b), 53.

18

(B) All other kinds of firearms[1] except—

   (*a*) prohibited weapons;[2]
   (*b*) air weapons not declared to be specially dangerous as above; and
   (*c*) smooth-bore guns (not being air guns) which—
      (*i*) have barrels not less than 24 inches long[3] and do not have any barrel with a bore exceeding 2 inches; **and**
      (*ii*) **either** have no magazine **or** have a non-detachable magazine incapable of holding more than two cartridges; **and**
      (*iii*) are not revolver guns.[4]

As to item (*ii*) above, a gun which has been adapted to have a non-detachable magazine will not fall within that item unless—

   (*a*) it bears an approved[5] mark denoting that it does so fall; **and**
   (*b*) that mark has been made, and the adaptation certified in writing as having been carried out in an approved[5] manner, by the Worshipful Company of Gunmakers of London, the Birmingham Proof House or by another approved[5] person.[6]

A weapon which—

(1) has at any time since 1st July 1989[7] been a weapon of a kind described at items (A) and (B) above, **or**
(2) would at any time before that date have been treated as a Section 1 firearm if the present legislation had then been in force,

---

[1] For the width of meaning of the term "firearm", see pp. 2–8.
[2] For the definition of "prohibited weapons", see pp. 11–12.
[3] For this measurement, see note 1 on p. 12.
[4] F.A. 1968 s. 1(1)(a), (3)(a); F.(A)A. 1988 s. 2(1)(2). For "revolver gun", see note 2 on p. 12.
[5] "Approved" means approved by the Secretary of State for the Home Office. The approved marks and the approved manner of adaptation may be found in *"Firearms Law: Specifications for the Adaptation of Shot Gun Magazines and the De-activation of Firearms"* obtainable from H.M.S.O. bookshops.
[6] F.A. 1968 ss. 1(3A), 58(1); F.(A)A. 1988 s. 2(3).
[7] The date on which F.(A)A. 1988 s. 2 came into force. (Firearms (Amendment) Act 1988 (Commencement No. 2) Order 1989, Article 3(a) and Schedule, Part I).

shall, if it has or at any time has had, a rifled barrel less than 24 inches long,[1] be treated as a Section 1 firearm notwithstanding anything done to convert it into a shot gun or an air weapon.[2] But, for the foregoing purposes, the shortening of a barrel by a registered firearms dealer[3] solely to replace part of it so as to produce a barrel not less than 24 inches long[1] shall be disregarded.[4]

A revolver discharging pellets propelled by compressed carbon dioxide is not an air weapon and therefore falls to be treated as a Section 1 firearm.[5]

Definition of Section 1 Ammunition

This classification is totally defined by exception. Section 1 applies to any ammunition for a firearm[6] except:

(a) Cartridges containing five or more shot, none of which exceeds 0.36 of an inch in diameter.
(b) Ammunition for an air gun, air rifle or air pistol.
(c) Blank cartridges not more than one inch in diameter.[7]

When Do I Need a Firearm Certificate?

Subject to the many exceptions[8] mentioned below, you need a firearm certificate if you purchase, hire, accept as a gift, borrow or have in your possession a Section 1 firearm or Section 1 ammunition.[9]

At this point it may be helpful to attempt some expla-

---

[1] For this measurement, see note 1 on p. 12.
[2] F.(A)A. 1988 s. 7(2). For the meaning of "air weapon", see note 4 on p. 51.
[3] As to the registration of firearms dealers, see pp. 137–140.
[4] F.(A)A. 1988 s. 7(3).
[5] *R. v. Thorpe* [1987] 2 All ER 108.
[6] That is, any firearm within the wide meaning of the definition discussed at pp. 2–8.
[7] F.A. 1968 s. 1(4). The one inch measurement is to be made immediately in front of the rim or cannelure of the base of the cartridge. (F.A. 1968 s.1(4)(c)).
[8] For two general exceptions to the need for a firearm certificate, see pp. 9–10.
[9] F.A. 1968 ss. 1(1), 57(4). The maximum punishment for non-compliance, on summary conviction, is imprisonment for 6 months or the statutory maximum fine (currently £2000) or both; or, on indictment, three years' imprisonment, or an unlimited fine, or both (F.A. 1968 s. 51(1)(2) and Schedule 6, Part I).

nation of the meaning of the word "possession" which is used here and which, with its cognate expressions, frequently occur in the following pages. The law itself admits that it has not yet been able to evolve a satisfactory definition of these terms! However, despite that admission, cases decided in the last 25 years have produced some guidance.

The words should be construed in a popular and not a narrow sense; a person has possession of an object, not only when carrying it, but also when the object is in some place, *e.g.*, a building or a vehicle, over which that person has control unless he does not realise that the object is, or may be, in that place.[1] Even control of the place where the object is may not be necessary; in a case concerning the need for a firearm certificate it was decided that the owner of firearms kept at his mother's flat in a different part of the country might still possess the firearms though not having physical custody of them.[2]

In a further case it was decided, perhaps predictably, that a person whose only interest in a firearm was to convey it from one person to another had possession of it during that time.[3] In another case the Court decided that the fact that the accused did not know that what he possessed was a firearm was immaterial; the offence is an absolute one.[4]

The latest court case on the question of possession has introduced a new concept of dual possession. C. had left two of his shot guns with T. for safekeeping while C. and T. went on holiday together and for later cleaning by T.

---

[1] *Lockyer v. Gibb* [1966] 2 All ER 653; *Warner v. Metropolitan Police Commissioner* [1968] 2 All ER 356.

[2] *Sullivan v. Earl of Caithness* [1976] 1 All ER 844.

[3] Woodage v. Moss [1974] 1 All ER 584. Note that if the person conveying the firearm had been a carrier in business as such or a registered firearms dealer in business as such, or acting as an employee of either, he would not have needed a firearm certificate—see items (1) and (2) on p. 22.

[4] *R. v. Hussain* [1981] WLR 416; *The Times*, 20th November 1980. The weapon in question was an 8 in. metal tube with a striker pin activated by a spring, capable of firing .32 cartridges.

The Court held that during that period C. had "proprietary possession" of the guns and T. had "custodial possession".[1]

The cases in which a firearm certificate is not needed for a Section 1 firearm are as follows:

(1) *Firearms Dealers*

The purchase, hiring, accepting as a gift, borrowing or possessing, in the ordinary course of business, of a firearm by a person carrying on the business of a firearms dealer, and registered as such, or by an employee of such a person.[2]

(2) *Auctioneers, Carriers and Warehousemen*

The possession,[3] in the ordinary course of business, of a firearm by a person carrying on the business of an auctioneer,[4] carrier or warehouseman, or by an employee of such a person.[5]

(3) *Slaughtering Instruments*

(*a*) The possession[6] by a licensed slaughterer[7] of a slaughtering instrument[8] in any slaughterhouse or knacker's yard in which he is employed.[9]

---

[1] *Hall v. Cotton and Another* [1986] 3 All ER 332. Whilst the point at issue concerning possession was possession by T., who held no shot gun certificate, it is evident that the court was of the view that there was concurrent possession by C.

[2] F.A. 1968 ss. 8(1), 57(4). As to firearms dealers and their registration, see pp. 137–140.

[3] Note that possession only is covered by this exemption, and not a purchase, hiring, accepting as a gift or borrowing.

[4] Auctioneers require a police permit to cover the sale by auction of firearms. See pp. 52–53.

[5] F.A. 1968 s. 9(1). Failure to take reasonable precautions for the safe custody of a firearm by persons of these descriptions, or to report forthwith any loss or theft to the police, is an offence. The maximum punishment is 6 months' imprisonment, or a fine at level 5 on the standard scale (currently £2000), or both (F.(A)A. 1988 s. 14).

[6] Note that possession only is covered by this exemption. A free certificate will be issued for the purchase or acquisition of a slaughtering instrument and ammunition (F.A. 1968 s. 32(3)(c)).

[7] *I.e.*, licensed under S.A. 1974 s. 39.

[8] A slaughtering instrument is defined as a firearm which is specially designed or adapted for the instantaneous slaughter of animals or for the instantaneous stunning of animals with a view to slaughtering them (F.A. 1968 s. 57(4)).

[9] F.A. 1968 s. 10(1).

(b) The possession[1] of slaughtering instruments[2] and ammunition for them for the purpose of storing them in safe custody at a slaughterhouse or knacker's yard by—
   (i) the proprietor of that slaughterhouse or knacker's yard; or
   (ii) a person appointed by the proprietor to take charge of those slaughtering instruments and ammunition for the purpose of such storage.[3]

(4) *Ships and Signalling Apparatus*
   (a) The possession[4] of a firearm on board a ship,[5] or the possession of signalling apparatus on board an aircraft or at an aerodrome, as part of the equipment of the ship,[5] aircraft or aerodrome.[6]
   (b) The removal of signalling apparatus, which is part of the equipment of an aircraft, or from or to an aircraft at an aerodrome to or from a place appointed for the storage of the apparatus in safe custody at that aerodrome; and the keeping of such apparatus at such a place.[7]
   (c) If a permit from a constable[8] is held for the purpose, the removal of a firearm from or to a ship[5] or signalling apparatus from or to an aircraft or aerodrome to or from such a place and for such purpose as is given in the permit.[9]

(5) *Carrying Firearms for Others*
The carrying of a firearm belonging to another person, who holds a firearm certificate, under instructions from, and

---

[1] See note 6 on p. 22.
[2] For the definition of this term, see note 8 on p. 22.
[3] F.A. 1968 s. 10(2).
[4] Note that possession only is covered by this exemption, and not a purchase, hiring, accepting as a gift or borrowing.
[5] The word "ship" includes hovercraft (Hovercraft (Application of Enactments) Order 1972, Art. 4, Sch. 1 Part A).
[6] F.A. 1968 s. 13(1)(a).
[7] F.A. 1968 s. 13(1)(b).
[8] See note 8 on p. 94 for the meaning of "constable".
[9] F.A. 1968 s. 13(1)(c); F.(A)A. 1988 s. 21(3).

for the use of, that other person and for sporting purposes only.[1]

(6) *Target Shooting Clubs*

The possession[2] by a member of a rifle club, miniature rifle club or pistol club approved by the Home Office[3] of a firearm when engaged as such a member in, or in connection with, target practice.[4]

Home Office approval may be limited to specified types of rifles or pistols. An approval will, unless withdrawn,[5] last for 6 years, and may be renewed for further 6-year periods. A fee of £33[6] is payable on its grant or renewal. A constable,[7] authorised for that purpose by a chief officer of police, may, on producing that authority if required, enter and inspect club premises to check whether the foregoing provisions are being complied with; it is an offence[8] to obstruct him.[9]

An approval of a rifle or miniature rifle club given by the

---

[1] F.A. 1968 s. 11(1). The shooting of rats is not shooting for sporting purposes only (*Morton v. Chaney* [1960] 3 All ER 632).

[2] Note that possession only is covered, and not a purchase, hiring, accepting as a gift or borrowing, for which a free certificate will be granted to a responsible officer of the club; the certificate may also be varied or renewed without charge. But if the approval of the club is limited to specified types of rifles or pistols, a free certificate will only be granted for those types (F.A. 1968 s. 32(2); F.(A)A. 1988 s. 15(8)).

[3] The procedure is for rifle clubs to apply individually to the local police for Home Office approval. This is generally done through the National Small-Bore Rifle Association or the National Rifle Association. Before approving a club the Home Office has to be satisfied, amongst other things, that the club will be responsibly run, that the ranges to be used are safe, and that there will be no danger to the public. The procedure for approval of pistol clubs is similar, the relevant association being the National Pistol Association. A Home Office leaflet entitled "*Approval of Gun Clubs*" is to be issued in 1989.

[4] F.(A)A. 1988 s. 15(1). F.A. 1968 s. 11(3) is now superseded in respect of rifle and miniature rifle clubs (F.(A)A. 1988 s. 15(7)).

[5] Though not so stated, it may be presumed that it would be open to the Home Office to withdraw an approval if a limitation on types of weapons, or the restriction on use of guns described in the last paragraph, were to be breached.

[6] This fee may be varied or abolished by Home Office order (F.A. 1968 s. 43(1); F.(A)A. 1988 s. 15(4)).

[7] See note 8 on p. 94 for the meaning of "constable".

[8] The maximum punishment on summary conviction is a fine at level 3 on the standard scale (currently £400) (F.(A)A. 1988 s. 15(6)).

[9] F.(A)A. 1988 s. 15(2)–(6).

Home Office before 1st July 1989[1] will expire 3 years after that date, but will be renewable.[2]

(7) Cadet Corps

The possession[3] by a member of a cadet corps approved by the Home Office[4] of a firearm when engaged as such a member in, or in connection with, drill or target practice.[5]

(8) Miniature Rifle Ranges and Shooting Galleries

(a) The purchase, hiring, accepting as a gift, borrowing or possessing of a miniature rifle[6] not exceeding .23 calibre by a person conducting or carrying on a miniature rifle range (whether for a rifle club or otherwise) or a shooting gallery at which in either case no firearms are used other than non-dangerous air weapons[7] or miniature rifles not exceeded .23 calibre.[8]

(b) The use by any person at any rifle range or shooting gallery described in item 8(a) above of the miniature rifles there described and ammunition for them.[9]

(9) Theatrical Performances

The possession[10] by a person taking part in a theatrical performance or any rehearsal thereof, or in the production

---

[1] The date on which F.(A)A. 1988 s. 15 came into force; The Firearms (Amendment) Act 1988 (Commencement No. 2) Order 1989. Approvals issued before this date will have been given under F.A. 1968 s. 11(3).

[2] F.(A)A. 1988 s. 15(9).

[3] Note that possession only is covered, and not a purchase, hiring, accepting as a gift or borrowing, for which a free certificate will be granted to a responsible officer of the corps; the certificate may also be varied or renewed without charge (F.A. 1968 s. 32(2); F.(A)A. 1988 s. 15(8)).

[4] The Home Office has given a general approval to all "recognised units" of the Combined Cadet Force, Sea Cadet Corps, Army Cadet Force and Air Training Corps.

[5] F.A. 1968 s. 11(3); F.(A)A. 1988 s. 15(7).

[6] The term "miniature rifle" is not defined in the Firearms Acts. Non-dangerous air weapons (for which see p. 18) may be used at the rifle range or shooting gallery without a firearms certificate.

[7] For these weapons, see p. 18.

[8] F.A. 1968 ss. 11(4), 57(4).

[9] F.A. 1968 s. 11(4).

[10] Note that possession only is covered, and not a purchase, hiring, accepting as a gift or borrowing.

of a film, of a firearm during, and for the purpose of, that performance, rehearsal or production.[1]

(10) *Starting Pistols*
The possession[2] of a firearm by any person at an athletic meeting for the purpose of starting races at that meeting.[3]

(11) *Police permits*
The possession,[2] in accordance with the terms of the permit, of a firearm by any person who holds a police permit.[4]

(12) *Military and Police Forces*
The possession[5] by certain Crown servants,[6] members of visiting military forces and by police officers of a firearm in their capacities as such servants, members or officers.[7]

(13) *Museums*
The possession, purchase, hiring, accepting as a gift or borrowing of firearms by a museum within the terms of a museum firearms licence.[8] Full details are contained in Chapter 8.

(14) *Borrowed Rifles*
The borrowing by a person aged 17[9] or more of a rifle[10]

---

[1] F.A. 1968 s. 12(1). This exemption may be taken to apply equally to television productions and rehearsals. As to the use of prohibited weapons on these occasions, see p. 00.

[2] Note that possession only is covered, and not a purchase, hiring, accepting as a gift or borrowing.

[3] F.A. 1968 s. 11(2). Though clearly intended to permit the use of starting pistols, s. 11(2) in fact allows the use of any firearm to start races.

[4] F.A. 1968 s. 7(1). As to police permits, see pp. 52–54.

[5] Possession only is covered by this exemption. In some of these cases a purchase, hiring, accepting as a gift or borrowing may be done without a certificate; in other cases a free certificate will be given.

[6] Principally, these will be members of the three fighting services. Others, such as customs officers, may be included.

[7] F.A. 1968 s. 54; Visiting Forces and International Headquarters (Application of Law) Order 1965.

[8] F.A. 1968 s. 57(4); F.(A)A. 1988 ss. 19, 25(1) and Sch., para. 1(2).

[9] As to the attainment of the age of 17, see note 1 on p. 117.

[10] "Rifle" is defined to include a carbine (F.A. 1968 s. 57(4); F.(A)A. 1988 s. 25(3)).

from the occupier of private premises[1] and the use of the
rifle there in the presence of[2] the occupier or his employee
if the occupier or his employee in whose presence the rifle
is used holds a firearm certificate for the rifle, and the
borrower's possession and use complies with any relevant
conditions in that certificate.[3]

(15) *Visitors' Permits*
The possession[4] of firearms by a holder of a visitor's
firearm permit.[5] Full details are contained in Chapter 7.

(16) *Firearms for Export*
The purchase of firearms for export purposes. The conditions under which this may be done are as follows: —

(i) the firearms must be bought from a registered firearms dealer;[6] **and**
(ii) the buyer shall not have been in Great Britain[7] for
more than 30 days[8] in the preceding 12 months; **and**
(iii) the firearms are to be bought for the purpose only
of being exported from Great Britain[7] without first
coming into the buyer's possession.[9]

Lastly, in connection with the need for a firearm certificate for a Section 1 firearm, it must be remembered that
the definition of "firearm" includes component parts of

[1] The term "private premises" is not defined in the Firearms Acts, though the
word "premises" includes any land (F.A. 1968 s. 57(4); F.(A)A. 1988 s. 25(1)),
and "land" includes land covered with water (Interpretation act 1978 s. 5 and Sch.
1). Contrasting the term with "public place", discussed on p. 128, it is suggested
that it means any land, water or buildings other than those to which the public
are admitted with or without payment.
[2] It remains for the Courts to decide how near the borrower must be to the
occupier or employee for this condition to be fulfilled.
[3] F.(A)A. 1988 s. 16(1).
[4] Note that possession only is covered, and not a purchase, hiring, accepting as
a gift or borrowing.
[5] F.(A)A. 1988 s. 17(1).
[6] As to the registration of firearms dealers, see pp. 137–140.
[7] "Great Britain" means England, Wales and Scotland, and excludes the Channel Islands and the Isle of Man.
[8] *I.e.*, a continuous period of 30 days, or an accumulated period of 30 days
composed of two or more shorter periods.
[9] F.(A)A. 1988 s. 18(1). The 1988 Act imposes certain duties on firearms dealers
selling firearms under these provisions (s. 18(2)–(4)), and these may be found on
p. 146.

firearms and their accessories designed or adapted to diminish noise or flash.[1] If you hold a component part or accessory, you should note the consequences of this, which are discussed on pages 7 and 8, and consult the police if in doubt

As with Section 1 firearms, there are numerous cases in which a firearm certificate is not needed for the handling of Section 1 ammunition. The cases are those in which under items (1), (2), (3), (5), (6), (7), (8), (11), (12), (13) and (15) on pages 22 to 27 a certificate is not needed for a Section 1 firearm.[2] A certificate is also unnecessary for ammunition for firearms and signalling apparatus under items (4)(*a*) and (*b*).[3] In the cases of items (9) and (10) a certificate will not be required since blank cartridges are not Section 1 ammunition.

In the case of item (14), a person borrowing a rifle may also, without holding a firearm certificate, purchase or acquire[4] ammunition for use in the rifle and may possess it during the borrowing if—

(*a*) the lender's firearm certificate authorises possession by the lender of the ammunition held by the borrower; **and**
(*b*) any conditions about ammunition in the lender's certificate are met by the borrower.[5]

In the case of item (15), the holder of a visitor's firearm permit may, as well as possessing Section 1 ammunition, also purchase or acquire[4] it.[6]

[1] See p. 6.
[2] F.A. 1968 ss. 7(1), 8(1), 9(1), 10, 11(1)–(4), 54, 57(4); F.(A)A. 1988 ss. 15, 17(1), 18(1), 19 and Schedule.
[3] F.A. 1968 s.13(1)(a), (b).
[4] "Acquire" means hire, accept as a gift or borrow (F.A. 1968 s. 57(4)).
[5] F.(A)A. 1988 s. 16(2).
[6] F.(A)A. 1988 s. 17(1).

How Do I get a Firearm Certificate?

You have to complete a form which is obtainable from a Police Station, and the application must be made to the chief officer of police for the area in which you reside.[1]

Three extra requirements, not formerly imposed, are now made by the Firearms Rules of 1989. Your personal particulars given on the application form must be verified by a person who —

(a) is not a member of your family; **and**
(b) is resident in Great Britain;[2] **and**
(c) has known you personally for at least two years; **and**
(d) is an MP, JP, minister of religion, doctor, lawyer, established civil servant, bank officer or other person of similar standing.[3]

Four up-to-date photographs are to accompany the application. One is to be signed by you and a second by the person verifying your personal particulars to the effect that the photograph is a current true likeness of yourself.[4]

The application must be signed by the person verifying your personal particulars to the effect that he knows of no reason why you should not be permitted to possess a firearm.[5]

You must state on the application form your reasons for needing the firearms and ammunition which you already hold and those intended to be acquired.[6]

These reasons are important because the 1968 Act stipulates that the police must, subject to the three specific reasons for refusal mentioned below, issue a certificate if

---

[1] F.A. 1968 s. 26(1). An applicant cannot be said to reside at a property which he has let (*Burditt v. Joslin* [1981] 3 All ER 203; *The Times*, 13th February 1981).
[2] For the meaning of "Great Britain", see note 7 on p. 27.
[3] F.A. 1968 s. 26(2)(b); Firearms Rules 1989, Rules 3(2), 5; Schedule 1, Part I. There is no other indication as to who the "person of similar standing" may be.
[4] F.A. 1968 s. 26(2)(a), (b); F.(A)A. 1988 s. 9; Firearms Rules 1989, Rules 3(3)(b), 7; Schedule 1, Part I.
[5] F.A. 1968 s. 26(2)(c); F.(A)A. 1988 s. 10; Firearms Rules 1989, Rules 3(3)(a), 6; Schedule 1, Part I.
[6] Firearms Rules 1989, Rule 3(1); Schedule 1, Part I.

satisfied that "the applicant has a good reason[1] for having in his possession, or for purchasing or acquiring,[2] the firearm or ammunition in respect of which the application is made, and can be permitted to have it in his possession without danger to the public safety or to the peace.[3]

The reasons given must be applicable to the type of firearm which you want to possess. For example, a certificate for a sporting rifle would not be granted unless you could show that you have, or are likely to have, some opportunity of using it for sporting purposes; and a certificate for a revolver with ammunition would seldom be issued unless you could show that you had regular and legitimate opportunity, *e.g.* as a member of a pistol shooting club, of using the weapon for target practice. The number of firearms to be covered by the certificate will be limited by the reasons for which they are required. Only in very exceptional cases will a certificate be given for firearms to be used to protect a person himself or his house; and this principle extends to banks and businesses who may wish to protect large quantities of valuables or money. Genuine collectors of firearms and ammunition, including those capable of use, will be regarded by the police as having a good reason for their possession.[4]

There are three cases in which the police must not grant a certificate.[5] These are, first, where the applicant is believed to be prohibited by the Act from possessing Section 1 firearms. This arises when the applicant has been given certain

---

[1] In deciding whether the applicant has a good reason, the police are exercising an administrative function with which the courts will be slow to interfere unless the police have acted in a capricious, arbitrary or unreasonable manner (*Hutchison v. Chief Constable of Grampian* 1977 SLT 98, Sheriff Ct.).

However, earlier cases, which were decided on similar provisions in the Firearms Act of 1937, appear to have ruled that the police must first consider this question from the point of view of an applicant, and not as possible objectors (*Anderson v. Neilans* [1940]; *Joy v. Chief Constable of Dumfries & Galloway* 1966 SLT 93, Sheriff Ct.).

[2] This means hiring, accepting as a gift or borrowing (F.A. 1968 s. 57(4)).

[3] F.A. 1968 s. 27(1). For a commentary on the meaning of "danger to the public safety or to the peace", see p. 44.

[4] As to Antique Firearms, see pp. 9–10.

[5] F.A. 1968, s. 27(1) proviso.

punishments by the Courts.[1] The second case is where the police have reason to believe the applicant to be of intemperate habits or unsound mind, and, thirdly, where they believe the applicant to be, for any reason, unfitted to be entrusted with the firearm. Examples of the last instance would be when the applicant is notoriously careless in the use of firearms, or liable to fits of uncontrolled temper in which he is dangerous.[2]

The certificate will specify particulars of the firearms already possessed and of those authorised by the certificate to be acquired,[3] and will give authority for the possession and acquisition of stated amounts of ammunition. On later purchases of firearms or ammunition, particulars are to be entered in the certificate or by the seller. A photograph of the holder of the certificate will be affixed to it.[4]

The certificate will last for three years,[5] unless previously revoked by the police[6] or cancelled by the Court,[6] and may be renewed every three years[5] by completing a further application form.[7]

---

[1] F.A. 1968, s. 21(1)–(3). These punishments are, briefly: (1) imprisonment, custody for life, preventive detention, corrective training, detention in a young offenders institution, youth custody, and young offenders discharged on licence. In some cases offenders are prohibited from possessing Section 1 firearms for life, in others for 5 years from release, and, in the last case, for the duration of the licence. (2) recognizance to keep the peace or to be of good behaviour, and probation, when made subject, in each case, to a condition that such firearms shall not be possessed, used or carried. The prohibition lasts for the duration of the punishment.

[2] Although these last two tests are different in terms from the second test applied in the case of shot gun certificates (see p. 44), the court decisions there cited may be of some relevance to the issue of firearm certificates.

[3] The exchange by a person with a firearms dealer of one firearm for another, even though similar, is not covered by that person's certificate unless it has been previously varied by the police to authorise the acquisition of the second firearm (*Wilson v. Coombe* QBD 29th July 1988; *Law Society's Gazette* 26 October 1988 at p. 44).

[4] F.A. 1968 s. 27(2); F.(A)A. 1988 ss. 9, 21(5).

[5] This period may be reduced by order made by the Home Office (F.A. 1968 s. 26(3)).

[6] As to revocation and cancellation, see pp. 33–34.

[7] F.A. 1968 s. 26(3); Firearms Rules 1989 Rule 3(1) and Schedule 1, Part I. The rules which govern the grant or refusal of the first certificate (see above) also apply on a renewal (F.A. 1968 s. 27(3)).

New legislation now permits arrangements for firearm certificates and shot gun certificates to be co-terminous.[1]

What else should I know about firearm certificates?

The certificate will be issued subject to a number of conditions.[2] Four will be imposed in all cases, and others[3] may be added by the police. The four are: —

(1) That the holder must, on the receipt of the certificate, sign it in ink with his usual signature.

(2) That the holder must at once inform the chief officer of police by whom the certificate was granted of the theft or loss in Great Britain[4] of any firearm to which it relates.

(3) That any change in the permanent address of the certificate holder shall be notified without undue delay to the chief officer of police by whom the certificate was granted.

(4) That, when the firearms and ammunition to which the certificate relates are in use[5] or transit, reasonable precautions must be taken for their safe custody; and that, at other times, they shall be stored securely so as to prevent, as far as reasonably practicable, access to them by unauthorised persons.[6]

---

[1] F.(A)A. 1988 s. 11.

[2] Failure to comply with a condition is an offence for which the maximum punishment on summary conviction is 6 months' imprisonment, or a fine at level 5 on the standard scale (currently £2000), or both (F.A. 1968 ss. 1(2), 51(1), (2) and Schedule 6, Part I).

[3] For example, that the firearms and ammunition shall only be used for certain purposes or on certain land. Extra conditions are also likely to be imposed when a certificate is issued for acting purposes.

[4] For the meaning of "Great Britain", see note 7 on p. 27.

[5] "Use" in this context includes occasions when a firearm is with the certificate holder for or in connection with its cleaning, repairing, testing, transfer or sale.

[6] Firearms Rules 1989, Rule 3(4) and Schedule 1, Part II. In a case decided under the former Firearms Rules 1969, which referred to "actual use", it was held that live ammunition concealed in the back of an unattended car for about half an hour is not in actual use nor kept in a secure place with a view to preventing access to it by unauthorised persons (*Marsh v. Chief Constable of Avon & Somerset, The Independent*, 8th May 1987, DC).

Any of the conditions, except those four just mentioned, may be varied by the police at any time, and they may require you to send them the certificate for alteration within twenty-one-days.[1] You may yourself apply to the police for it to be altered.[2] You should, for example, do this if the quantity or description of the firearms in your possession varies during the lifetime of a certificate, or if you want to hold or buy more ammunition than is authorised by the certificate.

The police may revoke your certificate for the same reasons as those for which they could have refused to grant it.[3] Your certificate can also be revoked if, when asked to do so, you fail to send it to the police for alteration of its conditions.[4]

If, in the first case, your certificate is revoked, the police may serve you with a notice requiring you to surrender it forthwith together with any firearms and ammunition which are in your possession by virtue of the certificate.[5] Failure to do so is an offence.[6]

If you successfully appeal against the revocation, the firearms and ammunition will be returned to you. If the appeal is dismissed, the Court can make an order for their disposal. If no appeal is made, or an appeal is abandoned, the firearms and ammunition will be disposed of in such manner as may be agreed between you and the police. In default of agreement, the police may decide on the method of disposal; but their decision must be notified to you and may be

---

[1] F.A. 1968, s. 29(1).

[2] F.A. 1968, s. 29(2). The usual application form is used for this purpose. (Firearms Rules 1989, Rule 3(1) and Sch. 1, Part I).

[3] F.A. 1968, s. 30(1)(a). For these reasons, see pp. 30–31.

[4] F.A. 1968, s. 30(1)(b). Upon conviction for failure to surrender, the maximum punishment is a fine at level 3 on the standard scale (currently £400) (F.A. 1968, s 51(1)(2) and Sch. 6, Part I).

[5] F.(A)A. 1988 s. 12(1).

[6] F.(A)A. 1988 s. 12(2). The maximum punishment on summary conviction is imprisonment for 3 months, or a fine at level 4 on the standard scale (currently £1000), or both.

appealed against to the Crown Court. The Court may either dismiss your appeal[1] or make its own order for disposal.[2]

If you are unfortunate enough to be convicted of any of certain offences or be given any of certain punishments[3] by a Court, the Court may cancel your certificate (or a shot gun certificate) and order any firearm or ammunition found in your possession[4] to be forfeited or disposed of. You must then, under threat of a further penalty,[5] surrender the certificate to the police within twenty-one days from the date of a notice from them to that effect.[6] Firearms and ammunition so forfeited may be seized and detained by the police who can, if the Court orders, destroy or otherwise dispose of them.[7]

You may appeal to the Crown court against the refusal

---

[1] In which case the police decision on disposal stands.

[2] F.A. 1968 s. 44; F.(A)A. 1988 s. 12(3)–(5). You should consult a solicitor if you are considering an appeal of either kind.

[3] The offences are any under the Firearms Act 1968 or the Firearms (Amendment) Act 1988, except an offence under s. 22(3) of the former Act (see p. 121) or offences relating specifically to air weapons (see pp. 121–123). The punishments are, briefly: imprisonment; detention in a young offender institution; detention in a detention centre or in a young offenders institution in Scotland; an order to enter into a recognizance to keep the peace or to be of good behaviour, a condition of which is that the offender shall not possess, use or carry a firearm; and probation with a requirement that the offender shall not possess, use or carry a firearm (F.A. 1968 s. 52(1), F.(A)A. 1988, s. 25(5)).

[4] The time of this finding is not specified. It is suggested that this must be at, or very shortly after, the commission of the offence for which one of the punishments in note 3 above has been given.

[5] The maximum fine on summary conviction is at level 3 on the standard scale (currently £400) (F.A. 1968 s. 51(1), (2) and Schedule 6 Part I).

[6] F.A. 1968 s. 52(2).

[7] The statements in this paragraph are qualified in the following cases:—

(a) In the case of air weapon offences (see pp. 121-123) and in the case of the offence of giving a shot gun or ammunition to a person under 15 (see p. 121), the Court's power to order forfeiture or disposal extends to guns and ammunition in respect of which the offence was committed as well as to those found in the convicted persons' possession.

(b) In the case of air weapon offences, in the case of illegal possession of a shot gun by a person under 15 (see p. 121), and in the case of any shot gun or ammunition in respect of which the offence of giving them to a person under 15 is committed, there is no power given to the police by the Act (though they may otherwise have it) to seize and detain either kind of gun or, subsequently, on the Court's order, to destroy or otherwise dispose of them (F.A. 1968 ss. 51(3), 52(2)–(4), 57(3), 58(4) and Schedule 6, Part I, and Part II, paras. 7–9).

of the police to grant you a certificate, or to vary or renew it, or against a revocation, unless it is revoked for the reason that you failed to send it to them for alteration of its conditions.[1]

A fee of £33 is payable on the grant or renewal of a certificate. The fee is £19 when a certificate is varied so as to increase the numbers of firearms to which it relates, except when the certificate is renewed at the same time. The replacement of a certificate which has been lost or destroyed costs £6.50.[2] No fee is charged for a certificate issued to a responsible officer of an approved rifle club, miniature rifle club, pistol club or cadet corps,[3] or for the variation or renewal of that certificate.[4] Fees are also dispensed with in cases relating to: firearms and ammunition required as part of the equipment of ships, hovercraft or their bases, aircraft or aerodromes; signalling apparatus and its ammunition so required for aircraft or aerodromes; signalling devices not more than 8 inches long when ready to fire and designed to discharge a flare, and ammunition for such devices; animal slaughtering instruments and their ammunition; and, where the certificate bears a condition that the firearm shall not be used, to "trophies of war".[5]

If you should be unwise enough to make a statement which you know to be false for the purpose of obtaining a certificate, or having it renewed or varied, whether for your-

---

[1] F.A. 1968 ss. 26(4), 29(2), 30(3), 44(1) and Schedule 5, Part II. The appeal must be made within 21 days after receipt of notice of the decision of the police. You should consult a solicitor if you are considering an appeal.

[2] F.A. 1968 s. 32(1), as amended by the Firearms (Variation of Fees) Order 1986.

These fees may be varied, or abolished altogether, by order made by the Home Office (F.A. 1968 s. 43(1)).

[3] As to the approval of cadet corps and similar forces and of rifle and pistol clubs, see note 4 on p. 25 and p. 24 respectively.

[4] F.A. 1968 s. 32(2); F.(A)A. 1988 s. 15(8). The firearms and ammunition covered by the certificate must be used only for target practice or drill by members of the clubs or corps.

[5] F.A. 1968 s. 32(3), (3A), (4); Hovercraft (Application of Enactments) Order 1972, Article 4, Sch. 1, Part A.

self or somebody else, you will be liable to be prosecuted and, if convicted, fined or sent to prison or both.[1]

Having a firearm certificate does not excuse you from obtaining a game licence when, according to the law, such a licence is necessary.[2]

If asked to do so, you must produce your certificate to a constable.[3] If you fail to do so, or to permit the constable to read the certificate, or to show him that you are entitled to hold the firearm or ammunition without a certificate,[4] the constable may seize and detain the firearm or ammunition and may require you to give him at once your name and address.[5]

You will commit an offence[6] if, with a view to purchasing or acquiring,[7] or procuring the repair, test or proof of, a Section 1 firearm or ammunition, you produce a false firearm certificate or such a certificate in which any false entry has been made, or impersonate a person to whom such a certificate has been granted or make any false statement.[8]

---

[1] F.A. 1968 ss. 26(5), 29(3), 51(1), (2) and Schedule 6, Part I. The maximum punishment is six months' imprisonment or a fine at level 5 on the standard scale (currently £2000), or both.

[2] F.A. 1968 s. 58(5). As to game licences, see pp. 68–76.

[3] F.A. 1968 s. 48(1). For the meaning of "constable", see note 8 on p. 94.

[4] I.e., demonstrate that your case comes within one of the exceptions mentioned on pp. 22–27.

[5] F.A. 1968 s. 48(2). If you refuse to give your name and address, or give them incorrectly, you will be liable upon summary conviction to a maximum fine at level 3 on the standard scale (currently £400) (F.A. 1968 ss. 48(3), 51(1), (2) and Schedule 6, Part I). Furthermore, you may be arrested without warrant if you make such a refusal, or if the constable suspects you of giving a false name or address or of "intending to abscond" (F.A. 1968 s. 50(3)).

[6] The maximum punishment on summary conviction is imprisonment for 6 months or the statutory maximum fine (currently £2000) or both; or, on indictment, 3 years imprisonment, or an unlimited fine, or both (F.A. 1968 ss 3(5), 51(1), (2) and Sch. 6 Part I).

[7] This word is defined as including letting or hire, giving, lending and parting with possession (F.A. 1968 2. 57(4)).

[8] F.A. 1968 s. 3(5).

Transferring Section 1 Firearms and Ammunition

You must not[1] sell or transfer[2] to any other person in the United Kingdom[3] a Section 1 firearm or Section 1 ammunition except in the following cases: —

(1) When "the other person" is a registered firearms dealer.[4]

(2) When "the other person" produces a firearm certificate authorising him to purchase or acquire[5] the firearm or ammunition,[6] or shows that he is entitled[7] to purchase or acquire[5] them without holding such a certificate.[8]

(3) A person may part with the possession of a firearm or ammunition, otherwise than in pursuance of a contract for sale or hire or by way of gift or loan, to another person who shows that he is entitled[7] to have possession of them without holding a firearm certificate.[9]

(4) When a firearm or ammunition is delivered by a carrier or warehouseman, or by an employee of either, in the ordinary course of his business or employment as such.[10]

---

[1] F.A. 1968 s. 3(2). The maximum punishment on summary conviction is imprisonment for 6 months or the statutory maximum fine (currently £2000) or both; or, on indictment, 3 years' imprisonment, or an unlimited fine, or both. (F.A. 1968 s. 51(1)(2) and Sch. 6 Part I).

[2] This word is defined to include let on hire, give, lend and part with possession. (F.A. 1968 s. 57(4)). The case of *Hall v Cotton and Another* [1986] 3 All ER 332 confirms that the leaving of a firearm with another person for safekeeping and cleaning is caught by this definition.

[3] "United Kingdom" means England, Wales, Scotland and Northern Ireland, and excludes the Channel Islands and the Isle of Man.

[4] As to the registration of firearms dealers, see pp. 137–140.

[5] This word is defined to mean hire, accept as a gift or borrow (F.A. 1968 s. 57(4)).

[6] A firearm certificate does not authorise the purchase or acquisition of a firearm bought or borrowed by way of exchanging it with another firearm unless the certificate specifically authorised that purchase or acquisition (*Wilson v. Coombe*, 24 July 1988, QBD; *Law Society's Gazette*, 26th October 1988 at p. 44).

[7] For the cases where a person would be so entitled, see pp. 22–28.

[8] F.A. 1968 s. 3(2).

[9] F.A. 1968 s. 8(2)(a).

[10] F.A. 1968 s. 9(4).

If you sell, let on hire, give or lend a Section 1 firearm or ammunition to any other person in the United Kingdom,[1] you must comply with any instructions in the firearm certificate produced;[2] and, in the case of a firearm, you must within 7 days of the transaction send by registered post or recorded delivery service notice of the transaction[3] to the chief officer of police by whom the certificate was issued.[4] But neither requirement need be met if "the other person" is a registered firearms dealer[5] or is entitled to purchase or acquire[6] the firearm or ammunition without holding a firearm certificate.[7]

You must not[8] by way of trade or business, unless you are a registered firearms dealer,[5] manufacture, sell, transfer,[9] repair, test, prove, expose for sale or transfer,[9] or possess for sale, transfer[9] repair, test or proof, any Section 1 firearms or ammunition.

You must not sell or transfer[9] **any** firearm or ammunition to any person whom you know, or have reasonable ground for believing, to be drunk or of unsound mind,[10] or to have been sentenced to certain punishments[11] by the Courts.[12]

---

[1] For the meaning of "United Kingdom", see note 3 on the previous page.

[2] *I.e.*, produced by the person to whom the transfer is made in accordance with item (2) on the last page. The prescribed form of certificate contains five standard instructions (Firearms Rules 1989, Schedule 1, Part II).

[3] The notice must contain a description of the firearm (including any identification number) and state the nature of the transaction and the name and address of the other person concerned.

[4] Failure to comply with either requirement is an offence the maximum punishment for which on summary conviction is imprisonment for 6 months or the statutory maximum fine (currently £2000) or both; or, on indictment, 3 years' imprisonment, or an unlimited fine, or both (F.A. 1968 ss. 42(2), 51(1), (2) and Sch. 6 Part I).

[5] As to the registration of firearms dealers, see pp. 137–140.

[6] For the cases where a person would be so entitled, see pp. 22–28.

[7] F.A. 1968 s. 42(1); F.(A)A. 1988 s. 23(6).

[8] F.A. 1968 s. 3(1). The maximum punishment is as given in note 1 on p. 37.

[9] This word is defined to include let on hire, give, lend and part with possession (F.A. 1968 s. 57(4)).

[10] F.A. 1968 s. 25. The maximum punishment on summary conviction is 3 months' imprisonment, or a fine at level 3 on the standard scale (currently £400), or both (F.A. 1968 s. 51(1)(2) and Sch. 6 Part I).

[11] These punishments are summarised in note 1 on p. 31.

[12] F.A. 1968 s. 21(5). The maximum summary punishment is as given in note 10 above. On indictment, the maximum is 3 years' imprisonment, or an unlimited fine, or both (F.A. 1968 s. 51(1)(2) and Sch. 6 Part I).

There are special restrictions on the handling of Section 1 firearms and ammunition by young people under 17; these are considered in Chapter 14 at pages 118 to 120. Further regulations are contained in the Firearms Act of 1968 about the holding of these firearms and ammunition by persons given certain punishments by the courts;[1] using firearms to endanger life, to injure property, to resist or prevent arrest[2] or with intent to commit an indictable offence;[3] and taking in pawn firearms and ammunition.[4] These, however, are matters which will not normally concern the average reader, and they are thus not dealt with further.

Work on Section 1 Firearms and Ammunition

You will commit an offence[5] if you undertake the repair, test or proof of a Section 1 firearm or ammunition for any other person in the United Kingdom[6] unless:—

(a) "the other person" is a registered firearms dealer;[7] **or**
(b) "the other person" produces, or causes to be produced, a firearm certificate authorising him to have possession of the firearm or ammunition, or shows that he is entitled[8] to have possession of it without holding such a certificate.[9]

You must not repair, prove or test **any** firearm or ammunition for any person whom you know, or have reasonable ground for believing, to be drunk or of unsound mind,[10]

---

[1] F.A. 1968 s. 21. These punishments are summarised in note 1 on p. 31.

[2] F.A. 1968 ss. 16, 17.

[3] F.A. 1968 s. 18.

[4] F.A. 1968 s. 3(6).

[5] The maximum punishment on summary conviction is imprisonment for 6 months or the statutory maximum fine (currently £200) or both; or, on indictment, 3 years' imprisonment, or an unlimited fine, or both (F.A. 1968 ss. 3(3), 51(1)(2) and Sch. 6 Part I).

[6] For the meaning of "United Kingdom", see note 3 on p. 37.

[7] See pp. 137–140 for the registration of firearms dealers.

[8] For the cases where a person would be so entitled, see pp. 22–28.

[9] F.A. 1968 s. 3(3).

[10] F.A. 1968 s. 25. For punishments, see note 10 on p. 38.

or to have been sentenced to certain punishments[1] by the Courts.[2]

Unless you are a registered firearms dealer,[3] you must not convert into a firearm anything which, though having the appearance of being a firearm,[4] is so constructed as to be incapable of discharging any missile through its barrel.[5]

It is an offence to shorten the barrel of a Section 1 firearm which is a smooth-bore gun[6] to a length of less than 24 inches[7] unless the barrel has a bore exceeding 2 inches. But a registered firearms dealer[3] may do so for the sole purpose of replacing a defective part of it so as to produce a barrel not less than 24 inches[7] long.[8]

---

[1] These punishments are summarised in note 1 on p. 31.

[2] F.A. 1968 s. 21(5). For punishments, see note 12 on p. 38.

[3] See pp. 137–140 for the registration of firearms dealers.

[4] For imitation firearms, see Chapter 9.

[5] F.A. 1968 s. 4(3). The maximum punishment on summary conviction is imprisonment for 6 months or the statutory maximum fine (currently £2000) or both; or on indictment, 5 years' imprisonment, or an unlimited fine, or both (F.A. 1968 s. 51(1)(2) and Sch. 6, Part I).

For a procedure for certifying that a firearm is incapable in this way, see p. 5.

[6] This will be a smooth-bore gun not falling within the description given in item (c) on p. 19.

[7] This measurement is to be taken from the muzzle to the point at which the charge is exploded on firing (F.A. 1968 s. 57(6)(a); F.(A)A. 1988 s. 25(1)).

[8] F.(A)A. 1988 s. 6. The maximum punishments for the offence are: on summary conviction, 6 months' imprisonment, or the statutory maximum fine (currently £2000), or both; on indictment, 5 years' imprisonment, or an unlimited fine, or both (F.(A)A. 1988 s. 6(1)).

CHAPTER 4

SHOT GUNS AND AMMUNITION

Definitions

The Firearms (Amendment) Act of 1988, substituting a new definition of "shot gun" for that formerly supplied by the 1968 Firearms Act,[1] defines that term to mean—

A smooth-bore gun (not being an air gun[2]) which—

(a) has a barrel not less than 24 inches long[3] and does not have any barrel with a bore exceeding 2 inches in diameter; and

(b) either has no magazine or has a non-detachable magazine incapable of holding more than two cartridges; and

(c) is not a revolver gun.[4]

As to paragraph (b) above, a gun which has been adapted to have a non-detachable magazine will not fall within the definition unless the conditions concerning approved marks

---

[1] By F.A. 1968 s. 1(3)(a).

[2] The term "air gun" is not defined by the Firearms Acts.

[3] This length is measured from the muzzle to the point at which the charge is exploded on firing (F.A. 1968 s. 57(6)(a); F.(A)A. 1988 s. 25(1)).

[4] F.A. 1968 s. 1(3)(a); F.(A)A. 1988 s. 2(1)(2). "Revolver gun" means a gun containing a series of chambers which revolve when the gun is fired (F.A. 1968 s. 57(2B); F.(A)A. 1988 s. 25(2)).

which are detailed in items (*a*) and (*b*) on page 19 are fulfilled.[1]

In certain circumstances, for which see page 13, a converted shot gun will fall to be treated as a prohibited weapon.[2]

No definition of shot gun ammunition is provided by the Firearms Acts. As we have seen,[3] ordinary shot gun ammunition is excluded from the kinds of ammunition which are classified as Section 1 ammunition.

When do I need a Shot Gun Certificate?

Shot gun certificates were introduced in 1968 to counter the increasing use of shot guns for criminal purposes. Briefly, the intention was to control the use of shot guns by means of certificates similarly to, but less strictly than, the ways in which rifles and hand guns had been controlled by firearm certificates for many years; shot gun ammunition is not, however, controlled by certificates.[4]

You will commit an offence[5] if you have in your possession[6] or purchase or acquire[7] a shot gun without holding a shot gun certificate,[8] but a certificate is not needed for the possession of component parts of a shot gun, nor in the following cases:[9]

(1) If you use a shot gun at a time and place approved

---

[1] F.A. 1968 ss. 1(3A), 58(1); F.(A)A. 1988 s. 2(1)(3).

[2] F.(A)A. 1988 s. 7(1).

[3] Item (*a*) on p. 20.

[4] Though production of a certificate is needed to buy shot gun ammunition.

[5] The maximum punishment on summary conviction is imprisonment for 6 months, or the statutory maximum fine (current £2000), or both or, on indictment, 3 years imprisonment or an unlimited fine, or both. (F.A. 1968 ss. 2(1), 51(1), (2) and Schedule 6, Part I).

[6] For some guidance on the meaning of "possession", see pp. 20–22.

[7] This word is defined to mean hire, accept as a gift or borrow (F.A. 1968 s. 57).

[8] F.A. 1968 s. 2(1).

[9] See also pp. 9–10 for two general exceptions to the need for a shot gun certificate.

for shooting at artificial targets by the chief Officer of Police for the area in which that place is situated.[1]
(2) If you hold a firearm certificate issued in Northern Ireland which authorises you to possess a shot gun.[2]
(3) If you borrow a shot gun from the occupier of private premises[3] and use it on those premises in the presence[4] of the occupier.[5]
(4) If you are able to bring your case within any one of the exceptions applying to firearm certificates which are numbered (1), (2), (4)(a) and (c), (5) (9), (10), (11), (12), (13) and (16) on pages 22–27 in Chapter 3. In the case of the exception numbered (5), the person for whom the shot gun is carried will require a shot gun certificate instead of a firearm certificate. Additionally, the holder of a visitor's shot gun permit[6] is entitled, without holding a shot gun certificate, to possess, purchase or acquire[7] shot guns.[8]

How Do I get a Shot Gun Certificate?

You have to fill in a form which is obtainable from your local Police Station, and the application must be made to the chief officer of police for the area in which you reside.[9]

The three new extra requirements for firearm certificate applications, as noted on page 29, also operate in the case

---

[1] F.A. 1968 s 11(6). It is important to note that the exception only operates whilst a gun is being used in this way at the approved time and place and will not cover the possession of a gun immediately before or immediately after such a use.

[2] F.A. 1968 s. 15.

[3] For commentary on the term "private premises', see note 1 on p. 27.

[4] It remains for the Courts to decide how near to you the occupier must be when you are using a gun. Meanwhile, it is suggested that if the occupier is at your side or perhaps in the same shoot as yourself the condition is fulfilled, but not otherwise.

[5] F.A. 1968 s. 11(5).

[6] For such a permit, see Chapter 7.

[7] "Acquire" means hire, accept as a gift or borrow (F.A. 1968 s. 57(4); F.(A)A. 1988 s. 25(1)).

[8] F.A. 1968 ss. 7(1), 8(1), 9(1), 11(1)(2), 12(1), 13(1), 54, 57(4); F.(A)A. 1988 ss. 16(1), 17(1), 18(1), 19, 25(1) and Schedule.

[9] F.A. 1968 s. 26(1); Firearms Rules 1989, Rule 4(1) and Schedule 2, Part I. As to residence, see note 1 on p. 29.

of a shot gun certificate application.[1] But reasons for having the gun are not required to be given on the application form; this appears to be a strange omission since, as mentioned below, the absence of a good reason will entitle the police to refuse the certificate.

The certificate will list particulars of the shot guns to be covered by it and provide for entries to be made when a gun is transferred. A photograph of the holder will be affixed to it.[2]

Except in the cases mentioned below, where the police cannot issue a certificate, a certificate will be issued to you if the police are satisfied that you can be permitted to possess a shot gun without danger to the public safety or to the peace.[3]

This criterion has been judicially considered on three occasions. In a 1974 case[4] it was held that it was right to refuse a certificate if there was a danger of the gun being misused in such a way that good order is disturbed, and poaching with the gun was cited as an example of that. But in 1978 a court decided that it was wrong to refuse a certificate on the grounds of a previous poaching conviction.[5]

Clearer guidance, albeit in general terms, has emerged as follows:

- (*i*) It is not necessary, in order to justify a refusal or revocation, for there to be a possibility of dangerous misuse.[2]
- (*ii*) The police must give individual consideration to each case.[3]
- (*iii*) It is right for the police to take account of the applicant's irresponsibility in other activities.[6]

---

[1] F.A. 1968 s. 26(1),(2); F.(A)A. 1988 ss. 9, 10; Firearms Rules 1989, Rules 4(1)–(3), 5, 6, 7 and Schedule 2, Part I.

[2] Firearms Rules 1989, Rule 4(5) and Schedule 2, Part II.

[3] F.A. 1968 s. 28(1); F.(A)A. 1988 s. 3(1).

[4] *Ackers and others v. Taylor* [1974] 1 All ER 771.

[5] *R. v. Wakefield Crown Court, ex parte Oldfield* [1978] Crim. L.R. 164.

[6] *Luke v. Little* 1980 SLT (Sh. Ct.) 138; a case in which the applicant had been convicted three times for drunken driving.

The cases in which the police cannot issue a certificate are if—

(a) they have reason to believe that you are prohibited by the Firearms Act of 1968 from possessing a shot gun;[1] **or**

(b) they are satisfied that you do not have a good reason for possessing, purchasing or acquiring[2] a shot gun.[3]

You will be regarded, in particular,[4] as having a good reason if the gun is intended to be used for sporting or competition purposes or for shooting vermin. An application is not to be refused by virtue of item (b) merely because you intend neither to use the gun yourself nor to lend it for anyone else to use.[5]

New legislation now permits arrangements for shot gun certificates and firearm certificates to be co-terminous.[6]

What else should I know about Shot Gun Certificates?

The same four conditions which are applied to firearm certificates[7] will apply to shot gun certificates, except that the conditions will not relate to shot gun ammunition. Also, the police may not add further conditions.[8]

---

[1] The cases in which you may be so prohibited from using a shot gun fall into two categories. First, when you have been sentenced by a court to various punishments other than a fine; the details are in F.A. 1968 s. 21(1)–(3) and are summarised in note 1 on p. 31. Secondly, if you are under 17, you are prohibited from possessing a shot gun in many cases; for details, see pp. 118–121.

[2] "Acquiring" is defined to mean hiring, accepting as a gift or borrowing (F.A. 1968 s. 57(4)).

[3] F.A. 1968 s. 28(1A); F.(A)A. 1988 s. 3(1).

[4] The use of the words "in particular" indicates that the purposes mentioned are to be accepted as good reasons and that other purposes may be so accepted. See, also, the considerations mentioned on p. 30 which may be relevant.

[5] F.A. 1968 s. 28(1B); F.(A)A. 1988 s. 3(1). This would apply where the gun is an heirloom or has some other sentimental value.

[6] F.(A)A. 1988 s. 11.

[7] For which see p. 32.

[8] F.A. 1968 s. 28(2)(a); Firearms Rules 1989, Rules 4(4), 5 and Schedule 2, Part II.

Failure to comply with any condition is an offence.[1]

A shot gun certificate will give the descriptions of the shot guns to which it relates (including, if known, the identification numbers of the guns), the makers' names and the gauge or calibre of the guns. A photograph of the holder will be affixed to it. The certificate will also provide for entries to be made in it recording details of any sale[2] or other transfer[3] of a shot gun to the certificate holder.[4]

The certificate will last for three years,[5] unless previously revoked by the police,[6] or cancelled by the Court,[7] and may be renewed every three years[5] for the same period by completing another application form.[8] A renewal may be refused for the same reasons as the grant of the original certificate may be refused.[9]

A fee of £12 is payable for the grant of a certificate and £8 for its renewal. The fee for the replacement of a certificate which has been lost or destroyed is £5.50.[10]

The rules which are applicable in the case of firearm certificates to cancellations, appeals,[11] surrenders on revo-

---

[1] The maximum punishment on summary conviction is imprisonment for 6 months, or a fine at level 5 on the standard scale (currently £2000), or both (F.A. 1968 ss. 2(2), 51(1)(2) and Schedule 6, Part I).

[2] "Sale" includes letting on hire.

[3] "Transfer" includes a gift or loan of a gun for more than 72 hours.

[4] F.A. 1968 s. 28(2A); F.(A)A. 1988 s. 3(2); Firearms Rules 1989, Rule 4(5) and Schedule 2, Part II. For the requirements imposed on the transferor of a shot gun to a certificate holder, see pp. 47–48.

[5] F.A. 1968 s. 26(3). This period may be reduced by order made by the Home Office (F.A. 1968 s. 26(3)).

[6] The police may revoke the certificate for either of the reasons (a) and (b) on p. 45 for which they are entitled to refuse to issue it (F.A. 1968 s. 30(2)).

[7] See p. 34 for the cases in which a certificate can be cancelled by a Court.

[8] F.A. 1968 ss. 26(3), 28; Firearms Rules 1989, Rule 4(1) & Sch. 2, Part I. The same form is used for original applications and for renewals. In the latter case the application is to be accompanied by the certificate to be renewed if it is available.
The renewal will be made subject to the same conditions as those applicable to the original certificate.

[9] F.A. 1968 s. 28(1).

[10] F.A. 1968 s. 32(1), as amended by the Firearms (Variation of Fees) Order 1986.

[11] Except that there can be no variation by the police of a shot gun certificate and thus no question of an appeal against such a variation arises.

cation or cancellation, the need for a game licence, false statements to obtain certificates, production of false certificates and impersonation, and production of certificates to the police also apply to shot gun certificates.[1]

Transferring Shot Guns and their Ammunition

Many of the restrictions on transferring Section 1 firearms and their ammunition, which were considered on pages 37 to 38, apply, some with modifications, to the transfer of shot guns and their ammunition. These are: —

(a) The sale or other transfer of firearms generally, but this does not apply to shot gun ammunition. The certificate required to be produced in the case of shot guns is a shot gun certificate.[2]

(b) The sale, transfer and other dealings with firearms and ammunition by way of trade or business, but this does not apply to shot gun ammunition.[3] It does, however, apply to component parts of shot guns and accessories for diminishing their noise or flash.[4]

(c) The sale or other transfer of firearms and ammunition to persons who are drunk or of unsound mind.[5]

Two sets of further restrictions have been added by the Firearms (Amendment) Act of 1988. If you sell, let on hire, give, or lend for more than 72 hours, a shot gun to another person in the United Kingdom[6] who is neither a registered firearms dealer[7] nor a person who shows that he is entitled[8] to purchase or acquire[9] the gun without holding a shot gun certificate, you must —

---

[1] F.A. 1968 ss. 3(5), 26(4), (5), 30(3), (4), 44(1), 48, 52, 58(5); F.(A)A. 1988 s. 12. As to these rules, see pp. 33–36.

[2] F.A. 1968 s. 3(2). See p. 37 for details.

[3] F.A. 1968 s. 3(1). See p. 38 for details.

[4] F.A. 1968 ss. 3(1), 57(4).

[5] F.A. 1968 s. 25. See p. 38 for details.

[6] For the meaning of "United Kingdom", see note 3 on p. 37.

[7] As to the registration of firearms dealers, see pp. 137–140.

[8] For the cases where a person would be so entitled, see pp. 42–43.

[9] "Acquire" is defined to mean hire, accept as a gift or borrow (F.A. 1968 s. 57(4); F.(A)A. 1988 s. 25(1)).

(1) comply with any instructions contained in the shot gun certificate[1] produced by the transferee; **and**

(2) within 7 days of the transaction—

(*i*) send a notice of it to the chief officer of police who issued your certificate; **or**

(*ii*) if you are entitled[2] to possess the gun without a certificate, send a notice of the transaction to the chief officer of police who issued the transferee's certificate.[3]

The transferee must within the same time send a notice of the transaction to the chief officer of police who issued his certificate.[4]

These notices of the transaction must—

(*a*) contain a description of the gun with any identification number it bears; **and**

(*b*) state the nature of the transaction and the name and address of the other person concerned; **and**

(*c*) be sent by registered post or recorded delivery service.[5]

It is an offence to fail to comply with any of the foregoing requirements.[6]

The second set of restrictions applies to ammunition which is not Section 1 ammunition[7] **and** which is capable of being used in a shot gun **or** in a smooth-bore gun to which that Section applies.[8]

---

[1] The prescribed form of certificate contains four standard instructions (Firearms Rules 1989, Sch. 2, Part II).

[2] For the cases where you would be so entitled, see pp. 42–43.

[3] F.(A)A. 1988 s. 4(1)(2). Both requirements under item (2), and that in the following paragraph, do not apply to the transfer of shot guns to or from a certificate holder whose certificate was granted or renewed before 1st July 1989 during the period for which the certificate was issued (Firearms (Amendment) Act 1988 (Commencement No. 2) Order 1989, Article 6).

[4] F.(A)A. 1988 s. 4(3). See note 3 above.

[5] F.(A)A. 1988 s. 4(4).

[6] The offence is punishable on summary conviction by a maximum of 6 months' imprisonment, or a fine at level 5 on the standard scale (currently £2000), or both (F(A)A. 1988 s. 4(5)).

[7] See p. 20 for what constitutes Section 1 ammunition.

[8] For smooth-bore guns within this description, see p. 19.

You will commit an offence[1] if you sell any such ammunition to a person in the United Kingdom[2] who is neither a registered firearms dealer[3] nor a person who sells it by way of trade or business, unless that other person—

(*a*) produces a firearm or shot gun certificate which authorises him to possess a shot gun or a smooth-bore gun to which Section 1 applies;[4] **or**

(*b*) shows that he is entitled[5] to possess such a gun without holding such a certificate; **or**

(*c*) produces such a certificate which authorises another person to possess such a gun, together with that person's written authority to buy the ammunition on his behalf.[6]

There are special restrictions on the handling of shot guns and their ammunition by young people under the age of 17; these are considered in Chapter 14 at pages 118–121.

Work on Shot Guns and their Ammunition

All of the restrictions about carrying out work on Section 1 firearms and their ammunition, which were considered on pages 39 to 40, apply to shot guns and their ammunition, but with one exception and one modification:

(*a*) The restrictions on shortening shot gun barrels, which are lastly mentioned on page 40, do not apply.[7]

(*b*) In the case of item (*b*) on page 39, the certificate to be produced will be a shot gun certificate.[8]

---

[1] The maximum punishments are as in note 6 on the previous page (F.(A)A. 1988 s. 5(3)).

[2] For the meaning of "United Kingdom", see note 3 on p. 37.

[3] As to the registration of firearms dealers, see pp. 137–140.

[4] For smooth-bore guns within this description, see p. 19.

[5] For the cases where he would be so entitled, see pp. 22–27.

[6] F.(A)A. 1988 s. 5(1)(2).

[7] But for similar restrictions on shot guns which are not Section 1 firearms, see the text below.

[8] F.A. 1968 ss. 3(1)(3), 4(3), 25.

It is an offence[1] to shorten the barrel of a shot gun to a length of less than 24 inches;[2] but a registered firearms dealer[3] may do so for the sole purpose of replacing a defective part of the barrel so as to produce a barrel of not less than that length.[4]

---

[1] The maximum punishment on summary conviction is imprisonment for 6 months, or the statutory maximum fine (currently £2000), or both; or, on indictment, 5 years' imprisonment, or an unlimited fine, or both (F.A. 1968 s. 4(1), 51(1)(2) and Sch. 6, Part I).

[2] This measurement is to be taken from the muzzle to the point at which the charge is exploded on firing (F.A. 1968 s. 57(6)(a)).

[3] See pp. 137–140 for the registration of firearms dealers.

[4] F.A. 1968 s. 4(1)(2).

CHAPTER 5

AIR WEAPONS AND AMMUNITION

As we have seen in Chapter 3,[1] the more powerful kinds of air weapons have been classified as specially dangerous, and these are treated as Section 1 firearms so that the rules in that chapter applying to those firearms apply equally to classified air weapons.

A revolver discharging pellets propelled by compressed carbon dioxide is not to be classified as an air weapon.[2] It therefore falls to be treated as a Section 1 firearm.

No definition for air weapon ammunition is supplied by the Firearms Acts. That ammunition is specifically excluded from the kinds which are to be treated as Section 1 ammunition.[3]

The only rules affecting the handling of air weapons which are not classified as specially dangerous[4] and air weapon ammunition are those which apply to young people under the age of 17, and these are described on pages 121 to 124.

---

[1] At p. 18.

[2] *R. v. Thorpe* [1987] 2 All ER 108.

[3] F.A. 1968 s. 1(4)(b).

[4] These kinds of air weapons are defined as air rifles, air guns and air pistols (F.A. 1968 ss. 1(3)(b), 57(4)).

CHAPTER 6

POLICE PERMITS

A police permit allows the holder to have in his possession[1] firearms and ammunition without holding a firearm certificate or a shot gun certificate.[2] Another form of police permit allows an auctioneer to sell by auction, expose for sale by auction and have in his possession for sale by auction firearms and ammunition without holding a certificate of either kind.[3]

Permits are obtainable from the chief officer of police for the area where the applicant resides or, as the case may be, for the area where the auction is to be held.[4]

A general permit will only be granted in special cases where it may not be necessary or desirable to issue a firearm certificate or a shot gun certificate and, in general, the duration of the permit will be short. A permit will, for example, be appropriate to authorise possession of firearms or ammunition by a person who has been refused a certificate, or has had it revoked, until he is able to dispose of them; or by a relative or executor of a deceased person or a receiver of a bankrupt's estate when firearms or ammunition form part of the property of the deceased person or bankrupt.

Here are two general forms of permit and two special forms for auctioneers, in each case one being for shot guns

---

[1] A purchase or other form of acquisition cannot be covered by a permit.
[2] F.A. 1968 s. 7(1). For these two kinds of certificate, see Chapters 3 and 4 respectively.
[3] F.A. 1968 s. 9(2). See also item (2) on p. 22 for the possession of firearms and ammunition by auctioneers and their employees. A third form of permit (prescribed by the Firearms Rules 1989 Rule 9(3) & Sch. 4, Part V) is available for handling firearms and signalling apparatus in connection with ships and aircraft; see, further, item (4)(c) on p. 23.
[4] F.A. 1968 ss. 7(1), 9(2).

and the other for Section 1 firearms and their ammunition. The latter, like a firearm certificate, gives full particulars of each firearm or type of ammunition; a shot gun permit describes each shot gun in the same way as a shot gun certificate. All permits bear a date of expiry.[1] All permits are likely to be issued subject to some or all of the following conditions[2]: —

(1) The person to whom the permit is granted shall inform the chief officer of police at once of the name and address of any person, except a registered firearms dealer,[3] purchasing or acquiring any of the firearms or ammunition listed in the permit.

(2) Reasonable precautions shall be taken to ensure the safe custody of the firearms and ammunition, and any loss or theft shall be reported at once to the chief officer of police.

(3) The permit shall be returned to the chief officer of police on or before the date on which it expires.

You should consult your local police station if you feel that the circumstances of your case call for the issue of a permit. No fee is payable, and there is no right of appeal against refusal by the police to grant a permit.

The use of a firearm or ammunition by a permit holder otherwise than in accordance with the terms and conditions of his permit will be an offence.[4] An offence is also committed if you make any statement which you know to be false

---

[1] Firearms Rules 1989, Rule 9(1)(2) and Sch. 4, Parts I–III. Neither the Firearms Act 1968 nor the Firearms Rules 1989 stipulate the duration of a permit, thus leaving that aspect to the police to decide in the light of the circumstances. A new permit can be sought on expiry. No forms of application for permits are prescribed, though police forms are available.

[2] The Firearms Rules 1969 (now revoked) prescribed the conditions to which permits would be subject. The 1989 Rules do not do so but allow for unspecified conditions to be imposed. Those conditions listed above are recommended in the publication *"Firearms Law: Guidance to the Police."* There is evidently no bar to further conditions being added.

Additionally, permits will bear a footnote requesting holders to report the loss of the permit to the local police at once.

[3] As to the registration of firearms dealers, see pp. 137–140.

[4] F.A. 1968 ss. 1(1), 2(1), 3(1)(b), 7(1), 9(2).

for the purpose of procuring, whether for yourself or another person, the grant of a permit.[1]

---

[1] F.A. 1968 ss. 7(2), 9(3). The maximum punishments upon summary conviction are 6 months' imprisonment, or a fine at level 5 on the standard scale (currently £2000), or both. For an offence connected with an auctioneer's permit, 3 years' imprisonment, or an unlimited fine, or both, may be imposed on indictment. (F.A. 1968 s. 51(1)(2) and Schedule 6, Part I).

CHAPTER 7

VISITORS' PERMITS

The Firearms Act of 1968 permitted visitors to this country to possess, purchase and acquire[1] a shot gun without holding a shot gun certificate.[2] No such provision was made in the case of other firearms. The 1968 Act provisions are now repealed[3] and replaced by new arrangements under the Firearms (Amendment) Act of 1988 which allow the grant of visitors' permits for those kinds of firearms for which a firearm or shot gun certificate would otherwise be required.

A visitor's firearm permit will permit the possession of Section 1 firearms[4] and the possession, purchase or acquisition[5] of such ammunition for firearms as is specified in the permit. A visitor's shot gun permit will permit the possession, purchase or acquisition[5] of shot guns.[6]

Applications for both kinds of permit may be made to the chief officer of police for the area in which the applicant resides[7] on behalf of the visitor named in the application. The police may[8] grant a permit if satisfied that: —
  (1) the person named in the application is visiting or intending to visit Great Britain;[9] **and**

---

[1] This means hire, accept as a gift or borrow. (F.A. 1968 s. 57(4)).

[2] F.A. 1968 s. 14. Some visitors were required to apply for a visitor's shot gun certificate.

[3] F.(A)A. 1988 s. 23(8).

[4] For the definitions of Section 1 firearms and ammunition, see pp. 18–20.

[5] The meaning of "acquisition" corresponds to that given in note 1 above.

[6] F.(A)A. 1988 s. 17(1); Firearms Rules 1989 Rule 8(3)(4) & Sch. 3, Parts III & IV. For the definition of "shot guns", see pp. 41–42.

[7] For a decision as to residence, see note 1 on p. 29.

[8] The police are not required to grant a permit even if satisfied on the matters stated above; nor if there is no bar to a grant under the provisions in the following paragraph. There is no right of appeal against refusal to issue a permit.

[9] For the meaning of "Great Britain", see note 7 on p. 27.

55

(2) the person has a good reason[1] for possessing, purchasing or acquiring[2] the firearms or ammunition for which the application is made while visiting Great Britain.[3]

But a permit will be refused if the police have reason to believe—

(a) that the person's possession of the weapons or ammunition in question would represent a danger to the public safety or to the peace;[4] **or**
(b) that the person is prohibited by the Firearms Act of 1968 from possessing those weapons or ammunition.[5]

A permit will be in force for the period stated in it which cannot exceed one year.[6]

Home Office rules[7] prescribe the form of permits, and conditions may be applied to them. A permit will specify the number and description of firearms to which it relates (including identification numbers if known) and the quantities of ammunition to be purchased, acquired[2] and held at any one time.[8] Conditions may be varied by written notice from the police to the permit holder; but no shot gun permit can have a condition imposed, initially or on variation, which restricts the premises where the shot gun or guns may be used.[9]

A single application (called a group application) may be made for the grant of a permit of either kind for a maximum

---

[1] For some considerations which may be relevant to "a good reason", see p. 30.

[2] "Acquiring" means hiring, accepting as a gift or borrowing. (F.A. 1968 s. 57(4); F.(A)A. 1988 s. 25(1)).

[3] F.(A)A. 1988 s. 17(2). For the meaning of "Great Britain", see note 7 on p. 27.

[4] For some comments on this criterion, see p. 44.

[5] F.(A)A. 1988 s. 17(3). For the cases where a person may be so prohibited, see pp. 30–31.

[6] F.(A)A. 1988 s. 17(6).

[7] See the Firearms Rules 1989 Rule 8(3)(4) & Sch. 3, Parts III & IV.

[8] F.(A)A. 1988 s. 17(4).

[9] F.(A)A. 1988 s. 17(5). Apart from this provision, the police are free to impose such conditions as they think fit. "*Firearms Law: Guidance to the Police*" 1989 recommends conditions similar to those imposed on police permits (see note 2 on p. 53); others, relevant to the occasions or locations of use, may be added.

of 20 permits for the visitors named in the application. The application must satisfy the police that the visitors' purpose in possessing the weapons in question while visiting Great Britain[1] is—

(1) using them for sporting purposes on the same private premises[2] during the same period;[3] **or**
(2) participating in the same competition or other event or the same series of competitions or other events.[4]

A fee of £12 is payable on the grant of a visitor's permit. In the case of a group application, when six or more permits are granted the fee will be £60 for all the permits.[5]

You will commit an offence if you make any statement which you know to be false for the purpose of obtaining a permit, or if you fail to comply with any condition in a permit.[6]

---

[1] For the meaning of "Great Britain", see note 7 on p. 27.

[2] For commentary on the term "private premises", see note 1 on p. 27.

[3] *E.g*, for a game shoot.

[4] F.(A)A. 1988 s. 17(7). The provisions mentioned earlier concerning refusal of permits, their validity and duration and the form of permits will apply to group applications and permits issued under them.

[5] F.(A)A. 1988 s. 17(8). It follows that, when five or less permits are granted, the fee will be £12 for each. These fees may be varied, or abolished altogether, by order made by the Home Office (F.A. 1968 s. 43; F.(A)A. 1988 s. 17(9)).

[6] The maximum punishment on summary conviction is 6 months' imprisonment, or a fine at level 5 on the standard scale (currently £2000), or both. (F.(A)A. 1988 s. 17(10)).

CHAPTER 8

MUSEUMS' FIREARMS LICENCES

The Firearms (Amendment) Act of 1988 contains new provisions enabling the Home Office to issue licences to certain museums authorising them to acquire and possess firearms for exhibition.[1] The museums to which these arrangements apply are set out in Appendix B at the end of the book.

An application for a museum licence should be made in writing to the Home Office (F8 Division) at 50 Queen Anne's Gate, London SW1H 9AT. There are no rights of appeal against a refusal to grant a licence. The making of a false statement to obtain a licence is an offence.[2]

A licence will authorise the persons responsible for the management of the museum[3] and their employees, without holding a firearm or shot gun certificate, to possess, and purchase or acquire,[4] for the purposes of the museum firearms and ammunition which are, or are to be normally, exhibited or kept at the museum or in particular parts of it which the licence may specify. A licence may also, in similar terms, cover prohibited weapons and prohibited ammunition[5] without the need to obtain the Home Office special authority which is normally required.[6]

---

[1] The new provisions are in s. 19 of, and the Schedule to, the Act.

[2] F.(A)A. 1988 Sch., para. 4(1)(a). The maximum punishment on summary conviction is 6 months' imprisonment, or a fine at level 5 on the standard scale (currently £2000), or both. (F.(A)A. 1988 Sch., para. 4(2)).

[3] These persons are defined to mean the museum's board of trustees, governing body or other person or persons (whether or not incorporated) exercising corresponding functions (F.(A)A. 1988 Sch., para. 6).

[4] "Acquire" means hire, accept as a gift or borrow (F.A. 1968 s. 57(4); F.(A)A. 1988 s. 25(1)).

[5] For the definitions of "prohibited weapons" and "prohibited ammunition", see pp. 11–14.

[6] F.(A)A. 1988 Sch., para. 1(2). As to the special authority, see p. 15.

A licence will not be granted or renewed unless the Home Office is satisfied, after consulting the police for the area in which the museum lies, that the arrangements for exhibiting and keeping the firearms and ammunition will not endanger the public safety or the peace.[1]

A licence may contain conditions to secure the safe custody of the firearms and ammunition.[2] The persons responsible for the management of the museum[3] commit an offence if they fail to comply with a condition, or if they cause or permit another person to do so,[4] but it will be a defence for them to prove that they took all reasonable precautions and exercised due diligence to avoid commission of the offence.[5]

A licence will be granted for a 5-year period[6] and can be renewed for successive 5-year periods.[6] It will continue in force for that time unless previously revoked or cancelled.[7] Revocation is effected by notice sent by the Home Office to the persons responsible for the management of the museum.[3] A licence can be revoked if—

(a) the Home Office are satisfied that the continuation of the exemption conferred by the licence[8] would result in danger to the public safety or to the peace;[9] **or**

(b) the persons responsible for the management of the

---

[1] F.(A)A. 1988 Sch., para. 1(3)(5). Whilst some of the matters reviewed on p. 44 in relation to endangering the public safety or the peace may be relevant, the Home Office's primary concern is likely to be the security arrangements for the firearms and ammunition. See, also, the following paragraph above.

[2] F.(A)A. 1988 Sch., para. 1(4). There is evidently no power to impose other conditions.

[3] For the definition of these persons, see note 3 on p. 58.

[4] F.(A)A. 1988 Sch., para. 4(1)(b). For maximum punishments, see note 2 on p. 58. Special provisions about offences by a body corporate may be found in para. 4(5) and (6) of the 1988 Act Schedule.

[5] F.(A)A. 1988 Sch., para. 4(4).

[6] The Home Office may by order substitute longer or shorter periods. (F.(A)A. 1988 Sch., para. 1(6)).

[7] F.(A)A. 1988 Sch., para. 1(5). A court convicting the licence holders of any of the offences mentioned in this chapter may order the cancellation of the licence. (F.A. 1968 s. 52(1); F.(A)A. 1988 s. 25(5)).

[8] *I.e.*, exemption from the need for a firearm or shot gun certificate or for an authority to hold prohibited weapons or ammunition, as the case may be.

[9] See note 1 above as to these dangers.

museum,[1] or any of their employees, have been convicted of an offence under the licensing provisions;[2]
or

(c) the persons responsible for the management of the
museum[1] have failed to comply with a notice requiring
them to surrender the licence on its variation by the
Home Office,[3] as described below.

A notice of revocation will require those persons to surrender the licence to the Home Office.[4] Failure to comply
is an offence.[5]

A licence may be varied by notice from the Home Office
in two ways: by varying its conditions, or by varying the
licence itself so as to extend or restrict the buildings to which
it applies.[6] The notice may require the persons responsible
for the management of the museum[1] to send the licence to
the Home Office for variation within 21 days of the date of
the notice.[7]

There is no right of appeal against the revocation or
variation of a licence.

The fee for the grant or renewal of a licence is £2000,
though the Home Office may reduce this in particular cases.
When a licence is extended to cover additional buildings,
the fee will be £75.[8]

The purchase, acquisition[9] or possession of antique fire-

---

[1] For the definition of these persons, see note 3 on p. 58.

[2] *I.e.*, any of the offences mentioned in this chapter.

[3] F.(A)A. 1988 Sch., para. 2(2)(3).

[4] F.(A)A. 1988 Sch., para. 2(4).

[5] The maximum punishment on summary conviction is a fine at level 3 on the
standard scale (currently £400). (F.(A)A. 1988 Sch., para. 4(3)).

[6] F.(A)A. 1988 Sch., para. 2(1).

[7] F(A)A. 1988 Sch., para. 2(2). Failure to return the licence is not made an
offence, but is one of the grounds on which the licence may be revoked; see item
(c) above.

[8] F.(A)A. 1988 Sch., para. 3(1). The amounts of the fees may be varied, or
abolished altogether, by Home Office order. (F.A. 1968 s. 43(1); F.(A)A. 1988
Sch., para. 3(2)).

[9] This word is defined to mean hiring, accepting as a gift or borrowing. (F.A.
1968 s. 57(4); F.(A)A. 1988 s. 25(1)).

arms by a museum as items of curiosity or ornament will not require a licence.[1]

---

[1] F.A. 1968 s. 58(2); F.(A)A. 1988 s. 25(6). See, further, pp. 9–10 where the difficulties of judging whether a firearm is an antique or not are considered.

CHAPTER 9

IMITATION FIREARMS

Increasing concern about the use of imitation firearms for criminal purposes, and uncertainty about the extent to which the 1968 Firearms Act applied to them,[1] led to the passing in 1982 of a new Firearms Act, which was brought into force on 1st November 1983. The expressed purpose of the Act is to apply (with some exceptions and qualifications) the provisions of the 1968 Act to imitation firearms if they fulfill certain conditions.[2]

An imitation firearm is defined, by reference to the 1968 Act, to mean anything which has the appearance of being a firearm (whether or not it is capable of discharging any shot, bullet or other missile) other than a weapon designed or adapted for the discharge of any noxious liquid, gas or other thing.[3]

The principal matters for consideration are: the conditions to be fulfilled if the 1968 Act is to apply; when it does apply, which of the Act's provisions then operate; and the defences available for offences involving imitation firearms.

There are two conditions, both of which must be fulfilled. Firstly, that the imitation firearm shall have the appearance of being a Section 1 firearm[4] In this context component parts and accessories are excluded.[5]

The second condition is that the imitation firearm shall

---

[1] See, for example, the cases discussed on pp. 4–6.

[2] F.A. 1982 s. 1 (2).

[3] F.A. 1968 ss. 5 (1) (b), 57 (4); F.A. 1982 s. 1 (3). See pp. 12–13 for weapons so designed or adapted.

[4] F.A. 1968 s. 1; F.A. 1982 s. 1 (1) (a), (4) (a); F.(A)A. 1988 s. 25 (7). For the definition of "Section 1 firearm" see pp. 18–20.

[5] F.A. 1968 s. 57(1); F.A. 1982 s. 1 (3), (4) (b).

be so constructed or adapted as to be readily convertible into a Section 1 firearm.[1] The 1982 Act goes on to say that the firearm shall be regarded as readily convertible if—

(a) it can be converted without any special skill on the part of the person converting it in the construction or adaptation of firearms of any descriptions; **and**

(b) the work involved in converting it does not require equipment or tools other than such as are in common use by persons carrying out works of construction and maintenance in their own homes.[2]

The Home Office explains that the equipment and tools referred to are taken to mean tools and equipment that are normally on sale in retail tools shops, do-it-yourself shops and from mail order supplier or discount catalogues. They include, the Home Office adds, electrically or hand-powered drills, with or without speed control and with or without a vibratory or hammer device, hacksaws, rotating abrasive discs and wheels, high speed twist drills, tungsten carbide masonry drills, hacksaw blades, hammers, drifts, punches, files, etc.[3]

If these two conditions are fulfilled, an imitation firearm will be subject to all the provisions of the 1968 Act which apply to firearms (other than those applying specifically to shot guns and air weapons), but excluding the provisions mentioned below.[4] The main effect is to require a firearm certificate to be obtained for the handling, etc., of imitation firearms in those circumstances where it would be needed for a real firearm, and the provisions described in Chapter 3 about certificates will apply,[5] as will the later provisions

---

[1] F.A. 1968 s. 1 (3); F.A. 1982 s. 1 (1) (b).

[2] F.A. 1982 s. 1 (6).

[3] Home Office leaflet *"Guidelines on the Design, Construction or Adaptation of Imitation Firearms"*.

[4] F.A. 1982 ss. 1 (2) (4), 2 (1).

[5] The Firearms Rules 1989 concerning certificates (for which, see pp. 29–33) have been amended so as to apply to imitation firearms (Firearms Rules 1989, Rule 2 (b)).

in that Chapter referring to Section 1 firearms.[1] An imitation firearm will also be a firearm for the purposes of Chapter 16.

The provisions of the 1968 Act which do not apply to imitation firearms (so far as those provisions are discussed in this book) are those dealing with—

(a) Conversion into a firearm of anything incapable of discharging a missile.[2]

(b) Carrying a firearm in a public place.[3]

(c) Trespassing with a firearm.[4]

(d) Police powers in connection with items (b) and (c) above.[5]

It follows, then, from what has been said above that, with the exclusions just mentioned, the provisions contained in Chapters 2, 3, 6, 7, 8, 14, 15 and 16 apply to imitation firearms meeting the required conditions in the same way as they apply to real firearms, unless the provisions refer specifically to shot guns or to air weapons. The same offences may be committed, and the exceptions to those offences, where relevant, will apply.[6]

The 1982 Act has added a new defence which is available in any prosecution involving an imitation firearm. It applies when the accused can show[7] that he did not know and had no reason to suspect that the imitation firearm was so constructed or adapted as to be readily convertible (as

---

[1] For measures which can be taken to prevent an imitation firearm from becoming subject to the 1982 Act, see the leaflet mentioned in note 3 on the previous page.

[2] F.A. 1968 s. 4 (3); F.A. 1982 s. 2 (2) (a). For such a conversion, see pp. 39–40.

[3] F.A. 1968 s. 19; F.A. 1982 s. 2 (3). For such a carrying, see pp. 127–129.

[4] F.A. 1968 s. 20 (1) (2); F.A. 1982 s. 2 (3). For such a trespassing, see pp. 129–130.

[5] F.A. 1968 s. 47 (1) (3)–(5); F.A. 1982 s. 2 (3). For these powers, see p. 130.

[6] F.A. 1982 ss. 1 (2), 2 (1).

[7] *I.e.*, can convince the court before whom he is prosecuted.

described on pages 62 to 63) into an imitation firearm to which the Act applies.[1]

In conclusion, it may assist to highlight in summary form the points to be considered in deciding whether an imitation firearm is to be treated as a firearm for the purpose of the 1968 Act's provisions:

(1) It must have the appearance of being a Section 1 firearm.

(2) Component parts and accessories of imitation firearms are excluded.

(3) It shall be readily convertible into a real firearm.

(4) It is not to be treated as a firearm in the cases (a) to (d) on page 64.

---

[1] F.A. 1982 s. 1 (5). Contrast this defence with the absence of a corresponding defence if the firearm is a real one under the ruling in *R. v. Hussain*; see note 4 on p. 21.

CHAPTER 10

SHOOTING GAME

What is meant by "Game"

There are several Acts of Parliament dealing with the shooting of game. In some the word is defined, but often in different ways; in others there is no definition. The definition, or lack of it, will be mentioned when each of the statutory provisions is dealt with.

It is sufficient at this stage to make two general points. First, that the word is not always given its everyday meaning; for example, rabbits are included in the definition in two of the Acts.[1] Secondly, that the expression will include, where appropriate, dead game[2] as well as live, and tame game as well as wild.[3]

Strictly speaking, deer cannot be regarded as game, but, since most of the law in this chapter applies to game and deer, both are dealt with in the one chapter. The law relating specifically to the shooting of deer may be found on pages 95 to 103.

---

[1] G.L.A. 1860 s. 2; P.P.A. 1862 s. 1.

[2] Though the Game Act 1831 does not apply to game killed abroad (*Guyer v. R.* (1889) 23 QBD 100).

[3] *Cook v. Trevener* [1911] 1 K.B. 9; 74 J.P. 469. But tame pheasants are not "game" within the meaning of the Night Poaching Act 1828 (*R. v. Garnham* (1861) 2 F. and F. 34).

When can I shoot Game?

There are, firstly and mainly, periods of the year, known as "close seasons", during which game[1] and deer[2] must not be shot.[3] These periods vary according to the bird or animal protected.[4] A table of close seasons is set out in Appendix C at the end of the book.

Furthermore, there are certain days and times, outside the close seasons, during which game must not be killed. First, game must not be killed on a Sunday or Christmas Day.[5] For this purpose game includes hares, pheasants, partridges, grouse, heath or moor game and black game.[6] Since the word "includes" is used, it is possible that other birds and animals may fall within the provision if for due reason they can be described as game.[7]

Beyond these different definitions of game, there is a further distinction, which may be important, between shooting out of season and shooting on Sunday or Christmas Day. This arises from the different words used in the 1831 Game Act; in both cases the words "kill or take" are used, but in the latter case there are added the words "or use any dog, gun, net, or other engine or instrument[8] for the purpose of

---

[1] For this purpose game are only pheasants, partridges, black game, grouse or red game, bustards or wild turkeys (G.A. 1831 s. 3)

[2] For this purpose deer are the species listed in Section 3 of Appendix C at the end of the book (D.A. 1963 s. 1 (1) and 1st Schedule; R.D.A. 1977 ss. 1, 2(2)).

[3] G.A. 1831 s. 3; D.A. 1963 s. 1 (1).
A general exception arises under A.A. 1947 ss. 98, 100 (4). In this instance Government Ministers may require a person having the right to do so to take steps to kill particular birds and animals which are causing damage, even though they may be out of season. The only animals which may presently be the subject of this requirement are deer, though other animals and birds may be nominated by Government order.
For special exceptions relating to deer, see pp. 96–97, and for the maximum punishment in the case of deer, see note 3 on p. 95.
In the case of game, the maximum penalty on summary conviction is a fine at level 1 on the standard scale (currently £50) for every head of game illegally taken.

[4] G.A. 1831 s. 3; D.A. 1963 s. 1 and 1st Schedule; R.D.A. 1977 ss. 1, 2 (2).

[5] G.A. 1831 s. 3. The maximum punishment on summary conviction is a fine at level 1 on the standard scale (currently £50).

[6] G.A. 1831 s. 2.

[7] But the word "includes" has been interpreted in some statutory contexts to mean exclusively the things mentioned after it.

[8] E.g., a snare.

killing or taking any game". A little thought will reveal the significance of this; for example, to shoot at and miss a pheasant on Christmas Day is an offence, but to do so on a week-day in midsummer is not.

Thirdly, there are restrictions on shooting game at night. You must not unlawfully[1] take or destroy any game[2] or rabbits at night[3] on any open or enclosed land.[4] By a later Act[5] this restriction was extended to include any public road, highway or path or the sides thereof and the openings, outlets or gates from any open or enclosed land leading onto any public road, highway or path.[6]

When do I need a Game Licence?

If you "take, kill or pursue, or aid or assist in any manner in the taking, killing or pursuing by any means whatever, or use any dog, gun, net, or other engine for the purpose of taking, killing or pursuing any game, or any woodcock, snipe, or any coney,[7] or any deer[8]", you will need a game licence.[9] Thus, for all practical purposes, but subject to the exemptions later mentioned, if you go after game at all, you need a licence.

The word "game" is not defined in this context, but the

---

[1] *I.e.* without having the game rights. Thus, a tenant not having these rights may be convicted under this provision for these activities on land within his tenancy (*Liversedge v. Whiteoak* (1893) 57 J.P. Jo. 692). The expression "unlawfully" would also, it seems, embrace the case where a game licence was required but was not held; as to the need for a game licence, *see* pp. 68–72.

[2] "Game" includes hares, pheasants, partridges, grouse, heath or moor game and black game; N.P.A. 1828 s. 13. As to "includes", *see* p. 67 and note 7 thereto.

[3] This is from one hour after sunset to one hour before sunrise; N.P.A. 1828 s. 12.

[4] N.P.A. 1828 s. 1. To do so is an offence with a maximum punishment on summary conviction of a fine at level 3 on the standard scale (currently £400). For an interpretation of "enclosed lands", though in another context, *see* p. 70.

[5] N.P.A. 1844 s. 1.

[6] For restrictions on night shooting by tenants having the right to kill ground game, *see* p. 115. As to shooting deer at night, *see* p. 97.

[7] *I.e.* rabbit.

[8] All ages and both sexes of deer are included (*R. v. Strange* (1843) 1 L.T. (O.S.) 435).

[9] G.L.A. 1860 s. 4.

Game Act 1831, which also provides an offence of not having a game licence when you ought to have one,[1] defines "game" for the purpose of that offence as including hares, pheasants, partridges, grouse, heath or moor game and black game.[2] Since the word "includes," is used, this list (plus, of course, woodcock, snipe, rabbits and deer) is not necessarily exhaustive.[3]

If you do any of the things described above for which a game licence is needed, without having taken out a licence which is still in force, you will be liable on summary conviction to a maximum fine at level 2 on the standard scale (currently £100).[4] It will also be an offence if you kill or take any game,[5] or use any dog, gun, net, "or other engine or instrument" for the purpose of searching for or killing or taking game without having a game licence;[6] the maximum fine in this case is at level 1 on the standard scale (currently £50).[7] Conviction for the latter offence provides no exemption from prosecution for the former offence,[6] though it is to be doubted whether the police, or another prosecutor, would doubly prosecute in this way.

Some examples taken from decided cases help to show the wide scope of the requirement for a licence. If you walk with a dog or a gun on land where there is game, or only point a gun at game, there is evidence of the commission of an offence.[8] From this it follows that if two or more of you fire at the same bird and the person killing it cannot be identified, each of you who has no licence will have committed an offence.[9] If you kill game by accident and take it

---

[1] G.A. 1831 s. 23.
[2] G.A. 1831 s. 2.
[3] But see note 7 on p. 67.
[4] G.L.A. 1860 s. 4.
[5] This includes hares, pheasants, partridges, grouse, heath or moor game and black game; G.A. 1831 s. 2. As to "includes" see p. 67 and note 7 thereto.
[6] G.A. 1831, s. 23 In the case of the first offence it will be a defence to show that you do not need a licence under one of the exemptions considered below; G.L.A. 1860 s. 5.
[7] G.A. 1831 s. 23.
[8] *R. v. Davis* (1795) 6 Term Rep. 177.
[9] *Hunter v. Clark* (1902) 66 J.P. 247.

away, you will also be guilty;[1] thus, if you knock over a pheasant with your car, stop, pick it up and put it in the car, and then drive on, you will have committed an offence if you have no game licence. If you are caught with game in your possession, it is up to you to prove that you acquired it innocently, *i.e.* in circumstances in which a licence is not needed.[2]

The cases in which a game licence is not needed for shooting are as follows[3]–

(1) The taking and killing of deer[4] in any enclosed lands by the owner or occupier of such lands, or by his direction or permission.[5] A decision in a court case usefully interprets two points on this exception. The lower court had decided that the meaning of "enclosed lands" was restricted to a deer park or other enclosure where deer were kept, but the higher court considered this to be too narrow a meaning and widened it to include "lands used for farming and enclosed by normal agricultural hedges" in contrast with "moorland where there are no enclosures and where the deer can run free". The second point established was that a game licence is not needed when a deer is shot on enclosed land where the shooter has the owner's permission even though the deer runs on and drops on land where he does not have that permission.[6]

(2) The taking or destroying of rabbits by the proprietor of any warren or of any enclosed ground

---

[1] *Molton v. Cheeseley* (1788) 1 Esp. 123.

[2] *Hemming v. Halsey* (1823) 1 L.J. (O.S.) K.B. 105.

[3] G.L.A. 1860 s. 5.

[4] For special restrictions on the shooting of deer, *see* Chapter 12.

[5] It seems that, to take advantage of this exception, the owner or occupier must have the right to take or kill deer on the land. Similarly, permission can only be given by whichever of the two has the right (*Halsbury's Laws of England*, 4th Edition, Vol. 2, para. 304, note 7).

[6] *Jemmison v. Priddle* [1972] 1 All E.R. 539.

whatever, or by the tenant of lands,[1] either by himself or by his direction or permission.[2]

(3) Shooting by the Royal Family and Her Majesty's gamekeepers.

(4) A person aiding or assisting in the taking or killing of game[3] in the company or presence of, and for the use of, another person who has a game licence in his own right, who is taking some active part in the shoot with his own dog or gun and who is not acting "by virtue of any deputation or appointment". The effect of this is to exempt beaters, loaders and other assistants from the necessity of being licensed; but such unlicensed beaters, etc., must not assist a gamekeeper since he holds his position by "deputation or appointment". Moreover, they apparently must not use or lend the use of any dog of their own, even to a licensed person who is by virtue of his licence then and there taking and killing game. Similarly, a loader may carry his employer's gun and thus aid in killing game, but he must not carry a gun of his own, and he must not fire either his own or his employer's gun.[4]

(5) The actual occupier of any enclosed lands,[5] or the owner thereof who has the right of killing hares on those lands, or a person authorised by either of them, may kill hares on those lands without a game licence, but not at night.[6] Any authority so given must be in writing and in the form given in the Act,

---

[1] *I.e.* any lands, whether enclosed or not.

[2] Some doubt exists as to whether both the proprietor and the tenant may permit another to take or destroy rabbits within this exception. Probably the latter only may do so (*Halsbury's Laws of England*, 4th Edition, Vol. 2, para. 304, note 6).

[3] As well as using the word "game" (which is not defined), this exemption extends to woodcock, snipe, rabbits and deer.

[4] *Halsbury's Laws of England*, 4th Edition, Vol. 2, para. 304, note 3; *Ex Parte Sylvester* (1829) 9 B & C 61.

[5] For an interpretation of "enclosed lands", *see* p. 70.

[6] H.A. 1848 ss. 1, 5; G.L.A. 1860 ss. 5, 6; "night" lasts from one hour after sunset to one hour before sunrise (H.A. 1848 s. 7).

or a form to the like effect.[1] This statutory form is as follows:–

> "I, A. B., do authorise C. D. to kill hares on ['my lands' or 'the lands occupied by me', as the case may be] within the
>   [here insert the name of the Parish or other place, as the case may be.]
>
> Dated this   day of
>
> Witness   (signed) A. B."

An owner or occupier may only give one authority at a time within one parish. The authority, or a copy, is to be registered with the clerk to the local magistrates. Once registered, it "shall be held good until after the first day of February,[2]" in the year following that within which it is granted unless revoked and notice of revocation given to the clerk to the magistrates. The registered authority, or the unrevoked register thereof, shall be sufficient evidence of the right of the person to whom the authority is given to kill hares on the lands mentioned in it without holding a game licence.[3]

(6) A person required by a Government Minister to kill certain animals and birds as pests need not hold a game licence to kill them.[4]

(7) An occupier of land, and certain persons who may be authorised by him in writing,[5] may kill hares and rabbits on that land.[6]

---

[1] H.A. 1848 s. 1 and Schedule.

[2] The meaning of the words quoted is hard to fathom. *Halsbury's Laws of England* in its 3rd Edition (now superseded) suggested that they meant "up to and including the first day of February."

[3] H.A. 1848 s. 2. These provisions are now practically obsolete in view of the provisions of the Ground Game Acts, as to which *see* Chapter 13.

[4] A.A. 1947 ss. 98, 100 (4). For further details of the requirement, *see* footnote 3 on p. 67.

[5] As to who these persons may be, *see* pp. 113–114.

[6] G.G.A. 1880 ss. 4, 8.

How do I get a Game Licence?

Game licences are obtained from any Post Office at which Money Order business is transacted. They are also obtainable from some District Councils.[1]

The licence must show the amount of duty charged and the proper christian and surnames and place of residence of the person to whom it is issued.[2] It will be dated on the day when it is actually issued[2] and will also show the time at which it is issued. It will be in force on the day of issue[2] and from the time of issue, so that an offence committed on the day of issue but before the time of issue is not condoned.[3] It continues in force until the end of the day on which it is stated to expire,[4] unless forfeited by the holder being convicted of trespassing in the daytime upon lands in search of game in England or Scotland.[5] It is not transferable.

Game licences are issued for different periods and at different prices as follows:–

To be taken out after July and before November and to expire on 31st July following	£6
To be taken out after July and before November and to expire on 31st October in the same year	£4
To be taken out after October and to expire on 31st July following	£4
Any continuous period of 14 days—known as an occasional licence	£2

---

[1] Department of the Environment Circular No. 143 of 1973.
[2] G.L.A. 1860 s. 16.
[3] G.L.A. 1860 s. 4. *Halsbury's Laws of England*, 4th Edition, Vol. 2, para. 305. *Campbell v. Strangeways* (1877) 3 C.P.D. 105.
[4] G.L.A. 1860 s. 16. *Halsbury's Laws of England*, 4th Edition, Vol. 2, para. 305.
[5] G.A. 1831 s. 30; Game (Scotland) Act 1832; G.L.A. 1860 s. 11.

A gamekeeper's licence[1] .... £4[2]

What else should I know about Game Licences?

If you are discovered doing anything the doing of which requires a game licence, the following classes of people are entitled to ask you[3] to produce your licence to them[4]:–

(i) An authorised officer of the local authority.[5]

(ii) Any lord or gamekeeper of the manor, royalty or lands on which you are;

(iii) Any person who has himself taken out a game licence;[6]

(iv) The owner, landlord, lessee or occupier of the land on which you are.

When asked to do so, you should produce your licence to the person at the time, permit him to read it, and to copy it or any part of it. The person has no right to keep the licence longer than is necessary to do all or any of these

---

[1] This is an annual licence expiring on 31st July and obtained by the game-keeper's employer. It excuses the gamekeeper from having an ordinary game licence, but lasts only for the duration of his employment as gamekeeper and is limited to use on land on which the employer has a right to kill game. On a change of gamekeeper during the currency of a gamekeeper's licence, the licence may be endorsed by the issuing authority in favour of the new employee without further charge in his favour for the remainder of the period of the licence (G.L.A. 1860 ss. 2, 7, 8, 9).

The wording of the Act indicates that this type of licence does not cover a gamekeeper for killing woodcock, snipe, rabbits or deer for which, strictly, an ordinary game licence is needed.

[2] G.L.A. 1860 s. 2; C.I.R.A. 1883 ss. 4, 5, as amended by the Fees for Game and Other Licences (Variation) Order 1968. The Treasury may make further alterations in these fees (L.G.A. 1966 s. 35 (2) and Schedule 3, Part II, para. 1).

[3] The demand, if not made on the land on which the person has been discovered doing the act for which a licence is necessary, must be made so immediately after he has left it as to form a part of the same transaction. (*Scarth v. Gardener* (1831) 5 C. and P. 38).

[4] G.L.A. 1860 s. 10.

[5] In the City of London the local authority is the Common Council, and else-where in London the borough council. Outside London it is the district council (L.G.A. 1972 s. 213).

[6] The licensed person making the demand is not under any obligation to produce his own licence (*Scarth v. Gardener* (1831) 5 C. and P. 38).

things. You may, it seems,[1] refuse to produce your licence provided you give to the person asking for it your full name and address and the place at which you took out the licence. If you do not have the licence with you, or do not possess one at all, you must give these particulars. If you refuse to do any of these things, or give any false or fictitious particulars, or produce a false or fictitious licence, you may be fined a maximum of £100.[2]

The holding of a £6 licence entitles you to sell game to a licensed dealer in game.[3] Otherwise, you commit an offence[4] if you sell[5] game[6] to anyone unless you yourself are a licensed game dealer, or unless you are selling hares killed by you, or by specified persons[7] authorised by you, on land which you occupy.[8]

In no case are you allowed to sell, or indeed buy, a game bird[9] after the expiration of ten days from the beginning of its close season;[10] of these ten days, one is inclusive and one exclusive so that, for example, in the case of partridges, a sale after 11th February is illegal. This rule does not apply to foreign game birds,[11] or to live birds bought or sold for rearing or exhibition purposes or for sale alive.[12] Hares and

---

[1] *Molton v. Rogers* (1802) 4 Esp. 215; *Scarth v. Gardener* (1831) 5 C. and P. 38.

[2] G.L.A. 1860 s. 10. The fine stated is the current maximum at level 2 on the standard scale.

[3] G.A. 1831 ss. 17, 25; G.L.A. 1860 s. 13.

[4] The maximum fine is at level 1 on the standard scale (currently £50) for each head of game sold (G.A. 1831 s. 25).

[5] Or if you offer game for sale. There is, of course, no offence if you give it away.

[6] The expression includes hares, pheasants, partridges, grouse, heath or moor game and black game (G.A. 1831 s. 2). As to "includes" see p. 67 and note 7 thereto.

[7] As to who these persons may be, *see* Chapter 13, pp. 113–114.

[8] G.G.A. 1880 ss. 1, 4, 8. There are other exemptions in favour of an innkeeper selling game for consumption in his own house, provided he obtains it from a licensed game dealer (G.A. 1831 s. 26), and in the case of persons authorised by a J.P. to sell game seized by a constable (P.P.A. 1862 s. 2; G.L.A. 1960 ss. 3 (4), 4 (1), 4 (4)).

[9] *I.e.* any of the birds listed in note 6 above.

[10] For close seasons, *see* Appendix C at the end of this book.

[11] *Guyer v. R.* (1889) 23 Q.B.D. 100.

[12] G.A. 1831 s. 4. The maximum penalty on conviction is at level 1 on the standard scale (currently £50) for each head of game.

leverets, unless imported, must not be sold or exposed for sale during the months of March to July inclusive.[1]

Ownership of Game and Neighbours' Rights

Whilst birds and animals are in a wild state they cannot be completely owned by anyone, but in the following three cases there can be a qualified ownership:–

(1) A person who lawfully takes, tames or reclaims a wild animal or bird may claim it as his property until it regains its natural liberty;[2]

(2) An owner of land has a right to the young of wild animals or birds born on his land until they can run or fly away;[3]

(3) A landowner also has the right[4] to shoot or otherwise take wild animals or birds whilst on his land.[5]

Tame or domesticated birds and animals may be owned; it is likewise with wild birds kept in captivity or tamed.[6] Special rules were made in 1968 about stealing wild creatures. The offence of stealing them is only committed if—

(1) they are domesticated, tamed or ordinarily[7] kept in captivity; or

(2) their carcase has been reduced into possession[8] by

---

[1] H.P.A. 1892 ss. 2, 3. The maximum penalty on conviction is at level 1 on the standard scale (currently £50); this probably applies to each head of game.

[2] *Grymes v. Shack* (1610) Cro. Jac. 662.

[3] *Case of Swans* (1592) 7 Co. Rep. 15b at 17b; *Blades v. Higgs* (1865) 11 HL Cas. 621.

[4] For the cases when this right will be shared with or let to a tenant, *see* Chapter 13.

[5] *Blades v. Higgs*, as above.

[6] *Oke's Game Laws* (5th Edition, 1912) p. 17.

[7] *E.g.* the offence can be committed whilst they are temporarily out of captivity.

[8] No statutory definition is given of the phrase "reduce into possession". It is suggested that this means the doing of some act by the other person to assert his ownership, *e.g.* putting the carcase in his game bag or car or hiding it in some place.

or on behalf of another person and possession of them has not since been lost or abandoned; or

(3) another person is in course of reducing them into possession.[1]

Rather difficult questions may arise when game (or other wild birds or animals) are put up on one person's land and are killed there or elsewhere. A person who puts up and kills game on another's land does not thereby own the carcase; it belongs to the person having the shooting rights over that land. But if you put up game on your land and kill it on or over another's land, the ownership is yours. Similarly, though for different reasons, if you, being a trespasser, start game on A.'s land, follow it on to B.'s land and there kill it, you are the owner of the game.[2] Mere ownership of the carcase will not necessarily entitle the owner to retrieve it, and he must take care that he does not commit the offence of trespassing in pursuit of game.[3] Simply to discharge your gun at game over your neighbour's land does not make you liable to this offence,[4] but personal entry to retrieve the game may do so. Unfortunately, the law on this point is confused, as is illustrated by the following four Court decisions:–

(1) M., on land where he had a right to shoot, shot at and killed a pheasant on the ground on adjoining land occupied by U. and over which M. had no shooting rights. M. then went on to U.'s land and picked up the pheasant. The Court decided that M. should be convicted of trespassing in pursuit of game, since the shooting and picking up were one transaction constituting the pursuit.[5]

(2) A pheasant rose from H.'s land and, when it was over T.'s land, H., being on his own land, shot at

---

[1] T.A. 1968 s. 4 (4). Upon conviction on indictment for the offence the maximum term of imprisonment is 10 years. (T.A. 1968 s. 7.)

[2] *Blades v. Higgs* (1865) 34 L.J.C.P. 286, and cases there cited.

[3] As to this offence, *see* pp. 81–85.

[4] Although, technically, you will be committing the civil wrong of trespass.

[5] *Osbond v. Meadows* (1862) 26 J.P. 439; 31 L.J.M.C. 238.

it. The pheasant fell on T.'s land. H. went on to
T.'s land to pick up the pheasant which was then
dead. The Court decided there was no offence.[1]

(3) T., one of a party shooting pheasants, saw pheasants that had been shot fall into the adjoining
wood of S. Two days afterwards T. went into S.'s
wood to pick up the pheasants believing them to
be dead. The Court decided that if the pheasants
were dead, or only if T. believed them to be dead,
there was no offence, but otherwise if the pheasants
were alive or believed to be alive.[2]

(4) R. stood on his own land and fired at and killed a
grouse sitting on the adjoining land of G. After 9½
hours R. went on to G.'s land to pick up the bird
which had in the meantime been picked up by
somebody else. The Court decided that the shooting and searching were connected and together constituted a pursuit of game. R. was therefore guilty,
and it mattered not whether the grouse was dead
or alive when searched for.[3]

In all cases the entry on the adjoining land without permission will constitute the civil wrong of trespass, as
opposed to the criminal offence of trespass in pursuit of
game. Permission to enter and retrieve game may, however,
not easily be obtained!

Shooting Game on the Foreshore and over Water

In general, the foreshore,[4] the bed of the sea for some
distance below low-water mark, and the beds of estuaries,
arms of the sea and tidal rivers are owned by the Crown.
In some cases the Crown has granted these lands to private
individuals. Whether or not such a grant has been made,
the only general rights of the public which may be exercised

---

[1] *Kenyon v. Hart* (1865) 29 J.P. 260; 34 L.J. (N.S.) M.C. 87.

[2] *Tanton v. Jervis* (1879) 43 J.P. 784.

[3] *Horn v. Raine* (1898) 62 J.P. 420; 67 L.J.Q.B. 533.

[4] *I.e.*, the land between the high and low water marks of ordinary tides.

in these areas are rights of fishing and of navigation and their attendant rights, *e.g.*, anchoring and mooring. Thus, the public has no general right of shooting or otherwise taking game and other birds and animals, though it is said that the Crown, where it is the owner, will acquiesce in the exercise of a right to shoot by the public when this causes no mischief or injury.

For a private individual to have the right of shooting in the areas mentioned he must be able to show—

(1) That he owns or has acquired a title to the land or to the right of shooting by long uninterrupted usage;[1] or

(2) That he is entitled to the benefit of a grant from the Crown of the land in question.[2]

Non-tidal waters are treated as if they were land not covered with water; for example, the right to shoot over a lake depends upon whether the area of the lake forms part of the land within the shooting. Where the land is bounded by a river or stream, the general rule is that the boundary of the land is the middle of the water.

---

[1] The acquisition of the right in this way is governed by strict legal rules and it is not, for example, sufficient for a claimant to say merely that he has shot over a particular stretch of foreshore for many years.

[2] *Halsbury's Laws of England*, 4th Edition, Vol. 14, paras. 253–264, and Vol. 49, paras. 307–308.

CHAPTER 11

POACHING

Introduction

Before dealing with the cases in which a poacher can be prosecuted,[1] the reader should know that physical and civil law remedies may be taken against him under the ordinary rules relating to trespass by the occupier[2] of the land, as well as a prosecution.[3] Very briefly, if you are on land where you have no right to be, the occupier[2] of that land may order you to leave at once. If you do not, he[4] may use just sufficient force to expel you. The occupier[2] may also sue you in the civil courts for any damage which you may do whilst trespassing and, if you are a persistent trespasser, may be able to obtain an injunction[5] against you.

Acts of Parliament have created a number of poaching offences whose ingredients and penalties vary according to

---

[1] A prosecution may be instituted by anyone, whether he is interested in the land trespassed on or not. (*Halsbury's Laws of England*, 4th Edition, Vol. 2, para. 280).

[2] And also the owner, even though he may not be the occupier.

[3] Though, where a prosecution for daytime poaching has been started, civil proceedings for trespass cannot be brought against the offender for the same act by a person at whose instance or with whose concurrence or assent the prosecution was instituted (G.A. 1831 s. 46).

[4] Or others under the direction of the occupier or owner, *e.g.* their employees.

[5] *I.e.* an order of the Court forbidding you to commit further trespass, the penalty for non-compliance usually being imprisonment.

80

whether the offences are committed in the daytime or by night, whether the poacher is alone or with others, whether or not he is armed, and whether he resists or co-operates when detected.

Poaching in the Daytime

If you "commit any trespass"[1] by entering or being[2] in the daytime[3] upon any land in search or pursuit of game[4] or woodcocks, snipes . . . or conies[5]", you will commit an offence.[6] If five or more of you together do the same thing, each of you will upon conviction be liable to a greater penalty.[7]

If you are caught in the circumstances just mentioned by any one of a number of specified persons, you must, if asked to do so, leave the land at once and supply your full names and address. The persons who are entitled to make these requests are:–

(1) The person having the right of killing game[4] on the land;

(2) The occupier of the land, whether or not he has the right of killing game on it;

(3) A gamekeeper or other servant of, or any person authorised by, either of the persons described in (1) and (2) above;

---

[1] *I.e.* entry without the prior permission of the occupier of the land or, where the shooting rights are held by some other person, of that other person (G.A. 1831 s. 30). It is for the accused person to prove that he had this permission (G.A. 1831 s. 42), but it need not apparently be in writing.

[2] An entry or presence by a person is necessary to constitute the offence. The sending of a dog on to the land is not enough. (*Pratt v. Martin* [1911] 2 K.B. 90.)

[3] This lasts from the beginning of the last hour before sunrise to the end of the first hour after sunset (G.A. 1831 s. 34).

[4] The word "game" includes hares, pheasants, partridges, grouse, heath or moor game and black game (G.A. 1831 s. 2). As to "includes", *see* p. 67 and note 7 thereto.

[5] *I.e.* rabbits.

[6] G.A. 1831 s. 30. The maximum penalty on summary conviction is a fine at level 1 on the standard scale (currently £50).

[7] G.A. 1831 s. 30. The maximum penalty on summary conviction is a fine at level 3 on the standard scale (currently £400).

(4) A police constable.

If you refuse to give your real name and address, or give such a general description of your place of abode "as shall be illusory for the purpose of discovery", or wilfully continue or return upon the land, you may be apprehended by the person making the request, or by anybody acting by his order and in his aid, and later charged before a magistrate.[1] Any of these persons may also demand from you any game[2] in your possession which appears to have been recently killed and, if this is not delivered to them, they may seize it from you for the use of the person entitled to it.[3]

If five or more of you together are found on land in search or pursuit of game,[4] woodcock, snipe or rabbits in the daytime,[5] one or more of you having a gun, and you prevent or try to prevent "by violence, intimidation or menace" any of the persons described in items (1) to (4) above from approaching for the purpose of requiring you to leave the land or giving them your particulars, you will commit a further offence.[6]

Poaching by Night

As we have seen in Chapter 10,[7] there are certain restrictions against shooting game at night. Additionally, Parliament has created a more serious offence to deal with armed trespass in pursuit of game by three or more persons. An

---

[1] G.A. 1831 ss. 31, 31A. You will be liable on summary conviction to a maximum fine at level 1 on the standard scale (currently £50).

[2] This will be "game" as defined in footnote 4 on p. 81. Thus the power of seizure will not extend to woodcock, snipe and rabbits which are the other birds and animals which may be the subject of daytime poaching. But *see also* the police powers of seizure mentioned on p. 85.

[3] G.A. 1831 s. 36.

[4] This will be "game" as defined in footnote 4 on p. 81.

[5] This lasts from the beginning of the last hour before sunrise to the end of the first hour after sunset (G.A. 1831 s. 34).

[6] G.A. 1831 s. 32. The maximum fine on summary conviction is at level 4 on the standard scale (currently £1000). If you aid or abet the commission of the offence, you are likewise liable. This is so even though you may be on a road, and not on the land being trespassed upon (*Stacey v. Whitehurst* (1865) 18 C.B. (N.S.) 344).

[7] Page 68.

offence is committed if persons in such numbers are or enter on any land[1] unlawfully[2] by night[3] for the purpose of taking or destroying game[4] or rabbits and any of them is armed[5] with a gun, crossbow, firearm, bludgeon or any other offensive weapon;[6] each of the party in these circumstances will be guilty.[7] It is not necessary that all of the party should enter the land; if all are associated for a common purpose and some enter while others remain near enough to assist, all of them may be convicted.[8] Nor is it necessary that all of them should be on land in the same ownership.[9] but they must have a plan in common;[10] and they may be convicted even though they may have abandoned their arms before being arrested.[11]

There are also the offences of unlawfully[2] by night:[3] taking[12] or destroying any game[4] or rabbits on any land; or entering[13]

---

[1] This includes any public road, highway or path and the sides thereof, and the openings, outlets and gates from any land into them. (N.P.A. 1844 s. 1.)

[2] *I.e.* without having any necessary permissions or the right to take game.

[3] This means from one hour after sunset to one hour before sunrise (N.P.A. 1828 s. 12).

[4] This includes hares, pheasants, partridges, grouse, heath or moor game, black game and bustards (N.P.A. 1828 s. 13). As to "includes", see p. 67 and note 7 thereto.

[5] If one of the party is armed, all are deemed to be so (*R. v. Goodfellow* (1845) 1 Car. & Kir. 724 C.C.R.).

[6] This can include a large stone (*R.v. Grice* (1837) 7 C. & P. 803) and, dependent upon the circumstances, a stick (*R. v. Fry & Webb* (1837) 2 Mood. & R. 42). A definition of "offensive weapon" appears elsewhere as "any article made or adapted for use for causing injury to the person, or intended by the person having it with him for such use by him" (P.C.A. 1953 s. 1 (4)).

[7] N.P.A. 1828 s. 9. The maximum punishments on summary conviction are 6 months' imprisonment, or a fine at level 4 on the standard scale (currently £1000), or both. Originally the offender could have been transported overseas for 7–14 years!

[8] *R. v. Whittaker and others* (1848) 2 Car. & Kir. 636 C.C.R.

[9] *R. v. Vezzell and others* (1851) 2 Den. 274 C.C.R.

[10] *R. v. Nickless* (1839) 8 C. & P. 757.

[11] *R. v. Nash & Weller* (1819) Russ & Ry. 386.

[12] Taking does not necessarily involve the offence of theft. It means, not to take away, but to catch, *e.g.*, catching game in a snare with a view to keeping or killing it. (*R. v. Glover* (1814) Russ. & Ry. 269, C.C.R.)

[13] Personal entry is necessary (*R. v. Pratt* (1855) 4 E. & B. 860); thus, the sending of a dog on to land to drive out game does not constitute entry. (*Pratt v. Martin* [1911] 2 K.B. 90.)

or being on any land[1] with any gun, net, engine[2] or instrument for the purpose of taking or destroying game.[3] Any person found upon land committing either of these offences may be arrested by any of the following people who may also arrest him in any other place to which he may have been pursued:–

(1) The owner or occupier of the land;

(2) The lord of the manor or reputed manor in which the land lies;

(3) Any gamekeeper or servant of any of the persons listed at (1) and (2);

(4) Any person assisting such gamekeeper or servant.

The person so arrested must be delivered as soon as possible into the custody of a police officer to be brought before the magistrates.

If the offender assaults, or offers any violence to, a person so authorised to arrest him with any gun, cross-bow, firearm, bludgeon, stick, club or any other offensive weapon[4] whatsoever, he commits an offence.[5]

The powers to demand and seize game, which have been discussed in relation to daytime poaching,[6] apply equally to these two offences of nocturnal poaching.[7]

---

[1] This includes any public road, highway or path, or the sides of them, and the openings, outlets and gates from any land into them (N.P.A. 1844 s. 1).

[2] The word "engine" includes a snare. (*Allen v. Thompson* (1870) LR 5 QB 336 at 339.)

[3] N.P.A. 1828 s. 1. The maximum punishment on summary conviction for this offence is a fine at level 3 on the standard scale (currently £400).

[4] For some meanings of "offensive weapon", *see* note 6 on p. 83.

[5] N.P.A. 1828 s. 2. The maximum punishments on summary conviction are 6 months' imprisonment or a fine at level 4 on the standard scale (currently £1000), or both.

[6] *See* p. 82.

[7] G.A. 1831 s. 36.

Poaching by Day or Night

If you obtain game[1] by unlawfully going on any land, in search or pursuit of game,[2] you will commit an offence.[3]

If you use[4] any gun, part of a gun, cartridges or other ammunition, or nets, traps, snares or other devices of a kind used for the killing or taking of game, for unlawfully killing or taking game,[1] that will also be an offence.[3]

A person who is an accessory[5] to either of the last two offences is liable to the same penalties as the offender himself.[3]

Powers of Police

The original statutes dealing with poaching contain a number of provisions enabling the police to stop and search suspected persons and their vehicles, to arrest suspected persons and to seize and detain things found on those arrested.[6] Whilst some of these provisions remain in force, others do not. Today, comprehensive provisions of general application authorising the police to exercise these powers, and to enter and search premises, are to be found in the Police and Criminal Evidence Act 1984.

---

[1] "Game" includes hares, pheasants, partridges, woodcocks, rabbits, snipe, grouse and black or moor game (P.P.A. 1862 s. 1). As to "includes", see p. 67 and note 7 thereto.

[2] "Unlawfully in search or pursuit of game" means a trespass by the offender on land of which he is neither the owner, nor occupier, nor the gamekeeper, nor the servant of either, nor having any *bona fide* right to kill the game thereon; the trespass being also without the consent of the owner, or of any person having the right to kill game there, or of any person having any right to authorise the offender to enter or be upon the land for the purpose of searching for or pursuing game (Hall v. Knox (1863) 33 L.J.M.C.1).

[3] The maximum penalty on summary conviction is a fine at level 3 on the standard scale (currently £400). Guns and ammunition in the offender's possession may also be forfeited by the Court (P.P.A. 1862 s. 2; G.L.A. 1960 s. 3 (2)).

[4] So far as this offence is concerned, a gun may be said to be used for these purposes, even though it has not been fired (*Gray v. Hawthorn* (1960) S.L.T. (Notes) 86).

[5] An accessory is, briefly, one who assists the offender before or after the commission of the offence.

[6] These statutes are: P.P.A. 1862 s. 2; G.L.A. 1960 ss. 1, 2, 4.

CHAPTER 12

PROTECTED BIRDS AND ANIMALS

Introduction

The law relating to the protection of wild birds and wild animals has been consolidated and extended by the Wildlife and Countryside Act of 1981. That Act has repealed the Protection of Birds Acts 1954 to 1967 and the Conservation of Wild Creatures and Wild Plants Act 1975. The protection given to birds remains substantially as it was before; but that given to animals is now wider in its scope, both in relation to the variety of wild life protected and the protective measures enacted. The 1981 Act's provisions extend to the Scilly Isles and the territorial waters adjacent to Great Britain.[1]

The 1981 Act has also amended the provisions for the protection of deer, seals and badgers.

In this Chapter discussion of the protective measures is confined to those which relate to shooting and to those wild animals which may be the subject of shooting.

---

[1] For the meaning of "Great Britain", see note 7 on p. 27, and for the extent of territorial waters, see note 4 on p. 104.

Wild Birds, and Wild Animals Generally

It is first necessary to look at a number of definitions which the 1981 Act uses. A wild bird is defined to mean any bird of a kind which is ordinarily resident in, or is a visitor to, Great Britain[1] in, a wild state, but does not include poultry or (except in the three cases later mentioned) any game bird. Within this definition, further terms are defined: "poultry" means domestic fowls, geese, ducks, guinea-fowls, pigeons and quails, and turkeys; a domestic duck and a domestic goose mean, respectively, any domestic form of duck or goose; "game bird" means any pheasant, partridge, grouse (or moor game), black (or heath) game or ptarmigan.[2]

A wild animal is defined as any animal (other than a bird) which is or (before it was killed or taken) was living wild.[2] As a matter of general law, the term "animal" includes any creature not belonging to the human race.

With the exceptions next considered, it is an offence[3] to kill or injure intentionally, or to attempt to kill or injure intentionally, any wild bird[4] or any of the following animals: all species of horseshoe and typical bats, bottle-nosed dolphins, common dolphins, common otters, harbour porpoises (otherwise known as common porpoises), wild cats, dormice, pine martens, marine turtles, walruses, whales and

---

[1] For the meaning of "Great Britain", see note 7 on p. 27.

[2] W.C.A. 1981 s. 27 (1).

[3] The maximum punishment on summary conviction in the case of any wild animal or in the case of a wild bird which is listed in Schedule 1 to the Act (for which see Appendix D at the end of the book) is a fine at level 5 on the standard scale (currently £2000). In the case of any other wild bird it is a fine at level 3 on the standard scale (currently £400). Where more than one animal or bird is involved in an offence, these maxima may be multiplied by the number so involved (W.C.A. 1981 ss. 1 (4), 21 (1), (2), (5)).

[4] In this instance "wild bird" does not include any bird which is shown to have been bred in captivity, and a bird is not to be treated as bred in captivity unless its parents were lawfully in captivity when the egg was laid (W.C.A. 1981 ss. 1 (6), 27 (2)).

red squirrels.[1] These animals collectively are referred to below as listed animals.

The exceptions to these offences are:

(1) A wild bird listed in Part I of Schedule 2 to the Act may be killed, or injured in the course of an attempt to kill it, outside the close season which is laid down for that bird,[2] except—

    (a) in Scotland on Sundays and Christmas Days, and

    (b) in England and Wales in any area prescribed for the purpose by Government order.[3]

The names of the birds so listed and the close seasons for them are given in Appendix E at the end of the book. Both may be varied by Government order, and orders may be made giving special protection to any listed bird which have the same effect as a close season for it.[4]

(2) A wild bird listed in Part II of Schedule 2 to the Act may be killed, or injured in the course of an attempt to kill it, at any time by "an authorised person", except in Scotland on Sundays and Christmas Days.[5] The names of the birds so listed are given in Appendix F at the end of the book. An authorised person is the owner or occu-

---

[1] W.C.A. 1981 ss. 1 (1), 9 (1), 18 (1), Schedule 5. The animals mentioned are all those in Schedule 5 which might conceivably be shot at intentionally; a smooth snake is also listed. The listing may be varied by Government order (W.C.A. 1981 s. 22 (3) (4)). In proceedings for an offence these animals will be presumed to have been wild unless the contrary is shown (W.C.A. 1981 s. 9 (6)).

[2] W.C.A. 1981 s. 2 (1).

[3] W.C.A. 1981 s. 2 (3). No areas have yet been prescribed for this purpose.

[4] W.C.A. 1981 ss. 2 (5)–(7), 22 (1). To check on whether orders have been made, enquiries should be made to the Department of the Environment, Tollgate House, Houlton Street, Bristol BS2 9DJ. Notice of the making of all orders must be published in the *London Gazette*, or in the *Edinburgh Gazette* for orders affecting Scotland (W.C.A. 1981 s. 26 (5)).

[5] W.C.A. 1981 s. 2 (2) (3). The listing may be varied by Government order (W.C.A. 1981 s. 22 (1)); as to checking, see note 4 above.

pier[1] of the land on which the killing or injuring occurs or any person authorised by that owner or occupier.[2]

(3) To prevent damage to crops, pasture, animal or human foodstuffs, livestock,[3] trees, hedges, banks or any works on land, Government Ministers may require the person having the right to do so to kill wild birds and wild animals causing such damage. Such a killing or an injuring of a wild bird or a listed animal is excused in these circumstances.[4]

(4) Any act done in pursuance of the provisions of the Animal Health Act 1981 or of any order made under it is excused.[5]

(5) The killing of a wild bird or listed animal if it is shown[6] that it had been so seriously disabled, otherwise than by an unlawful act[7] of the killer, that there was no reasonable chance of its recovering.[8]

(6) Any act done if it is shown[6] that the act was the

---

[1] An occupier, in relation to land other than the foreshore, includes any person having any right of hunting, shooting, fishing or taking game or fish (W.C.A. 1981 s. 27 (1)).

[2] W.C.A. 1981 s. 27 (1). Certain local authorities and other statutory bodies may also authorise persons for this purpose. A written authority is not required by the Act but is advisable for the authorised person's protection from prosecution. An authorisation for this purpose does not confer a right of entry on land.

[3] For the meaning of "livestock", see note 6 on p. 90.

[4] A.A. 1947 s. 98; W.C.A. 1981 ss. 4 (1) (a), 10 (1) (a). A similar procedure operates in Scotland.

[5] W.C.A. 1981 ss. 4 (1) (b) (c), 10 (1) (b). This does not apply in all instances to wild birds listed in Schedule 1 to the 1981 Act, for which see Appendix D at the end of the book.

[6] I.e., if the person prosecuted for the offence can convince the court.

[7] The extent of the meaning of "unlawful act" is unclear. As well as meaning an act which is unlawful under the 1981 Act, the term may include acts which are otherwise unlawful; e.g., the illegal use of the gun which caused the disablement.

[8] W.C.A. 1981 ss. 4 (2) (b), 10 (3) (b).

incidental result of a lawful operation[1] and could not reasonably have been avoided.[2]

(7) The killing or injuring by an authorised person[3] of a wild bird (except one included in Schedule 1 to the Act[4]) or a listed animal if it is shown[5] that that was necessary for the purpose of preventing serious damage to livestock,[6] foodstuffs for livestock,[6] crops, vegetables, fruit, growing timber or fisheries.[7]

But, in the case of a listed animal, this exception will not apply if it had become apparent before the time of killing or injuring that that would prove necessary for the purpose of preventing serious damage of any of the kinds described, and **either** —

(a) a licence[8] authorising the action had not been applied for as soon as reasonably practicable after that fact had become apparent; **or**

(b) an application for a licence had been determined.[9]

(8) The killing or injuring by an authorised person[3] of

---

[1] *E.g.*, an accidental killing or injuring of a wild bird or listed animal by a moving vehicle or by a shot lawfully fired at something else.

[2] W.C.A. 1981 ss. 4 (2) (c), 10 (3) (c). But if the act is to affect a bat which is not in the living area of a house, the Nature Conservancy Council (whose address is 19–20 Belgrave Square, London SW1X 8PY) must be notified and allowed reasonable time in which to advise upon whether the act should be done and the method used (W.C.A. 1981 s. 10 (5)). But there is no compulsion to follow that advice.

[3] For the meaning of "authorised person", *see* item (2) on pp. 88–89.

[4] For the birds listed in Schedule 1, see Appendix D at the end of the book.

[5] *I.e.*, if the person prosecuted can convince the court.

[6] "Livestock" includes any animal which is kept: for the provision of food, wool, skins or fur; for the purpose of its use in the carrying on of any agricultural activity; or for the provision or improvement of shooting or fishing (W.C.A. 1981 s. 27 (1)).

[7] W.C.A. 1981 ss. 4 (3) (c), 10 (4). In the case of a listed animal, serious damage to any other form of property is included in the list.

[8] For licences, see item (9) below.

[9] W.C.A. 1981 s. 10 (6). This is a rather curious provision in that the exception will not be invalidated if the licence application is refused; it is only necessary to apply for a licence in good time.

a wild bird (except one included in Schedule 1 to the Act[1]) if it is shown[2] that that was necessary for the purpose of preserving public health, or public or air safety, or preventing the spread of disease.[3]

(9) Any killing or injuring of a wild bird or listed animal, or an attempt to kill or injure either, which is done under and in accordance with the terms of a licence granted by the appropriate authority.[4] Licences are obtainable only for special particularised purposes, and those which may be relevant to shooting are listed at Appendix G at the end of the book with details of the authority from whom they can be obtained.[5]

It is an essential ingredient of the offences of killing or injuring a wild bird or listed animal, or attempting to do so, that there was an intent to kill or injure. Therefore, if there is no such intent, no offence is committed.

The Wildlife and Countryside Act 1981 creates a number of other offences which are connected directly or indirectly with shooting, and these, together with the available defences, will now be considered.

It is an offence[6] intentionally to disturb any wild bird included in Schedule 1 to the 1981 Act[7] while it is building a nest or is in, on or near a nest containing eggs or young, or intentionally to disturb the dependent young of such a bird.[8] Similarly, it is an offence[6] intentionally to disturb any listed animal while it is occupying a structure or place which

---

[1] For the birds listed in Schedule 1, see Appendix D at the end of the book.

[2] *I.e.*, if the person prosecuted for the offence can convince the court.

[3] W.C.A. 1981 s. 4(3) (a), (b).

[4] W.C.A. 1981 s. 16 (1)–(3).

[5] Game birds, for which see p. 87, may be the subject of a licence (W.C.A. 1981 ss. 16, 27 (1)).

[6] The maximum punishment on summary conviction is a fine at level 5 on the standard scale (currently £2000) (W.C.A. 1981 ss. 1 (5), 21 (1) (a)). See, also, the last part of note 3 on p. 87.

[7] The birds included in Schedule 1 are listed at Appendix D at the end of the book. The Schedule 1 listing may be varied by Government order (W.C.A. s. 22 (1)).

[8] W.C.A. 1981 s. 1(5). Note 4 on p. 87 applies to this offence.

it uses for shelter or protection.[1] Attempts to disturb intentionally in these three cases are likewise made offences.[2]

The exceptions listed at items (4) and (6) on page 89 apply to all these offences, and disturbance of a bird or animal as the result of such a requirement by the Ministry of Agriculture as is mentioned in item (3) on page 89 will also be an exception.[3]

The 1981 Act prohibits many methods of killing wild birds and wild animals. There are three lists of these methods. One list applies to the kinds of wild animal which are described in Schedule 6 to the Act; their names are reproduced in Appendix H at the end of the book.[4] The remaining lists apply to all wild birds and to all wild animals respectively. Some duplication in the listing makes it more convenient to present the prohibited methods in the four groupings which appear below.

The lists of prohibited methods may be varied by Government order.[5] The use of a prohibited method is an offence[6] unless approved by a licence issued by the appropriate authority.[7] The prohibited methods, so far as they relate or may relate to shooting, are as follows:

(1) METHODS APPLYING TO ALL WILD BIRDS[8] AND TO WILD ANIMALS[9] IN SCHEDULE 6

    (a) Using for the purpose of killing—

---

[1] W.C.A. 1981 s. 9 (4) (b).

[2] W.C.A. 1981 s. 18 (1). Note 6 on p. 91 above applies.

[3] W.C.A. 1981 ss. 4 (1), (2) (c), 10 (1), (3) (c). In the case of a listed animal, its disturbance within a dwellinghouse is also excused but, if the animal is a bat not within the living area of a house, the provisions concerning the Nature Conservancy Council mentioned in note 2 on p. 90 must be followed (W.C.A. 1981 s. 10 (2) (5)).

[4] The listing may be varied by Government order (W.C.A. 1981 s. 22 (4) (a)).

[5] W.C.A. 1981 ss. 5 (2), 11 (4).

[6] The maximum punishment on summary conviction is a fine at level 5 on the standard scale (currently £2000). (W.C.A. 1981 ss. 5, 11, 21 (1) (2)). See, also, the last part of note 3 on p. 87.

[7] W.C.A. 1981 s. 16 (1) (3). See Appendix G at the end of the book for the purposes for which licences may be obtained.

[8] Game birds, for the meaning of which see p. 87, are included in this instance (W.C.A. 1981 ss. 5, 27 (1)).

[9] In any proceedings for an offence the animal in question shall be presumed to have been wild unless the contrary is shown (W.C.A. 1981 s. 11 (5)).

    (i) any automatic or semi-automatic weapon,[1]

    (ii) any device for illuminating a target or any sighting device for night shooting,

    (iii) any form of artificial light or any mirror or other dazzling device.

(b) For the purpose of killing, using as a decoy any sound recording.

(c) Using any mechanically propelled vehicle[2] in immediate pursuit of a bird or animal for the purpose of killing it.[3]

(2) METHODS APPLYING TO ALL WILD BIRDS[4]

(a) Using, for the purpose of killing, any shot gun of which the barrel has an internal diameter at the muzzle of more than $1^3/_4$ inches.

(b) For the purpose of killing, using as a decoy any live bird or other animal whatever which is tethered, or which is secured by means of braces or other similar appliances, or which is blind, maimed or injured.[5]

(3) METHOD APPLYING TO ALL WILD ANIMALS[6]

Using as a decoy, for the purpose of killing any wild animal, any live mammal or bird whatever.[7]

---

[1] "Automatic weapon" and "semi-automatic weapon" do not include any weapon the magazine of which is incapable of holding more than two rounds (W.C.A. 1981 s. 27 (1)).

[2] The word "vehicle" includes aircraft, hovercraft and boat (W.C.A. 1981 s. 27 (1)).

[3] W.C.A. 1981 ss. 5 (1) (c)–(e), 11 (2) (c)–(e).

[4] Game birds, for the meaning of which see p. 87, are included in this instance (W.C.A. 1981 ss. 5, 27 (1)).

[5] W.C.A. 1981 s. 5 (1) (c) (iv), (d).

[6] In any proceedings for an offence the animal in question shall be presumed to have been wild unless the contrary is shown (W.C.A. 1981 s. 11 (5)).

[7] W.C.A. 1981 s. 11 (1) (c).

(4) METHOD APPLYING TO WILD ANIMALS[1] IN SCHEDULE 6[2]

Using any mechanically propelled vehicle[3] in immediate pursuit of an animal for the purpose of driving it.[4]

The 1981 Act makes it an offence[5] if a person, for the purpose of committing any of the offences which have been described, has in his possession[6] anything capable of being used for committing one of those offences.[7] Many things so capable may be innocently possessed. It is suggested that the safeguard lies in the need for the prosecution for this offence to establish to the magistrates' satisfaction that the object in question was possessed for the purpose described; to that end, the prosecution would have to adduce evidence to demonstrate a link between possession and the commission, or intended commission, of one of the offences.

Constables,[8] who with reasonable cause suspect that a person is committing or has committed an offence under the Act, may without warrant stop and search the person, search and examine things the person has or is using, arrest him on failure to give a proper name and address, and seize and detain things which may be evidence of an offence or which may be forfeited by a convicting court.[9] Constables may also enter land (but not a house) to exercise these powers if they reasonably suspect that an offence is being committed.[10]

---

[1] In any proceedings for an offence the animal in question shall be presumed to have been wild unless the contrary is shown (W.C.A. 1981 s. 11(5)).

[2] The names of the animals in Schedule 6 are shown in Appendix H at the end of the book.

[3] The word "vehicle" includes aircraft, hovercraft and boat (W.C.A. 1981 s. 27 (1)).

[4] W.C.A. 1981 s. 11 (2) (e).

[5] The maximum punishment on summary conviction will be the same as that for the offence for the purpose of committing which possession is alleged (W.C.A. 1981 ss. 18 (2), 21 (1) (2)).

[6] For commentary on the meaning of "possession", see pp. 20–22.

[7] W.C.A. 1981 s. 18 (2).

[8] As well as police constables, including special police constables, the word "constables" includes others holding that office, e.g., harbour constables. The hallmark of a constable is his attestation as such before, usually, a J.P.

[9] W.C.A. 1981 s. 19 (1). For police powers of general application, see p. 85

[10] W.C.A. 1981 s. 19 (2).

As well as imposing fines, a convicting court is compelled to order the forfeiture of any bird or animal in respect of which the offence was committed. The court **may** also order forfeiture of any vehicle,[1] animal, weapon, or other thing which was used to commit the offence.[2]

Deer

CLOSE SEASONS

There are close seasons for four species of deer, and these are shown in Section 3 of Appendix C at the end of the book.

It is an offence[3] wilfully[4] to kill deer[5] of these species, or to attempt to do so, during their respective close seasons,[6] except where one of the following defences is available. One of these defences is available only to "an authorised person", and this means—

(a) the occupier of the land on which the action is taken; or

(b) any member of the occupier's household[7] normally resident on the occupier's land, and acting with the occupier's written authority; or

---

[1] The word "vehicle" includes aircraft, hovercraft and boat (W.C.A. 1981 s. 27 (1)).

[2] W.C.A. 1981 s. 21 (6).

[3] The maximum punishment on summary conviction is a fine at level 4 on the standard scale (currently £1000), or 3 months' imprisonment, or both (D.A. 1963 s. 6 (1)). If an offence involves more than one deer, the maximum fine shall be regarded as if there was a separate offence against each deer (D.A. 1963 s. 6 (2)).

[4] This means deliberately and intentionally, and not by accident or inadvertence (*R. v. Senior* (1899) 1 Q.B. 283 at pp. 290–91).

[5] The word "deer" will include deer of either sex and all ages (*R. v. Strange* (1843) 1 Cox C.C. 58), and tame deer as well as wild deer.

[6] D.A. 1963 ss. 1 (1) (4), 4 (1).

[7] As to such membership, see note 1 on p. 114. Though that note is derived from the law relating to ground game, it may serve as a guide pending any court decision on the words' meaning in the text above.

(c) any person in the ordinary service[1] of the occupier on the occupier's land, acting as above; or

(d) any person having the right to take or kill deer on the land on which the action is taken; or

(e) any person acting with the written authority of a person at (d) above.[2]

The defences are:–

(A) That the deer was killed or taken, or was injured in an attempt to kill or take it, by an authorised person by means of shooting, and the act was done on any cultivated land, pasture or enclosed woodland.[3] But this defence cannot be relied upon unless the authorised person shows[4] that—

   (i) he had reasonable grounds for believing that deer of the same species were causing, or had caused, damage to crops, fruit, growing timber or any other form of property on the land;[5] **and**

   (ii) it was likely that further damage would be so caused **and** such damage was likely to be serious; **and**

   (iii) his action was necessary for the purpose of preventing any such damage.[6]

(B) That the killing or attempting to kill was done for the purpose of preventing suffering by an injured or diseased deer.[7]

---

[1] As to "ordinary service", *see* note 3 on p. 114. Though that note is derived from the law relating to ground game, it may serve as a guide pending any court decision on the words' meaning in the text above.

[2] D.A. 1963 s. 10A (6).

[3] D.A. 1963 s. 10A (1).

[4] *I.e.*, convinces the court before whom he is prosecuted.

[5] *I.e.*, the land upon which the act was done, being land of one of the three descriptions given earlier in the text.

[6] D.A. 1963 s. 10A (3). For restrictions on the types of gun and ammunition which the authorised person may use, *see* item (2) on p. 98 and item (C) on pp. 99–100.

[7] D.A. 1963 s. 10 (1).

(c) That the killing or attempting to kill was done in pursuance of a Government Minister's requirement under Section 98 of the Agriculture Act 1947.[1]

(d) That the deer was killed by a person, or his authorised servant or agent, and that person, by way of business, kept the deer on land enclosed by a deer-proof barrier for the production of meat or other foodstuffs or skins or other by-products, or as breeding stock; and the deer so kept was conspicuously marked so as to identify it as kept by that person.[2]

KILLING DEER AT NIGHT

It is an offence[3] wilfully[4] to kill a deer[5] at night,[6] or to attempt to do so,[7] except where one of the defences described at (B) or (C) above is available.[8]

USE OF UNLAWFUL METHODS AND ILLEGAL POSSESSION OF OBJECTS

Subject to the defences later described, which are available in the instances below which are asterisked, the following acts done in relation to deer,[5] and attempts to commit those acts,[9] are offences[3]:–

(1) Using, for the purpose of killing any deer, any trap, snare, or poisoned or stupefying bait, whether or not it is of such a nature or so placed as to be

---

[1] This is a reference to Ministers' powers to require the person having the right to do so to kill deer (and other animals and birds) which are causing damage, even though they may be out of season.

[2] D.A. 1963 s.10(2A); D.A. 1987 s.1. This defence, added in July 1987, enables deer kept on deer farms to be killed and sold out of season.,

[3] For punishments, see note 3 on p. 95.

[4] For the meaning of "wilfully", see note 4 on p. 95.

[5] For the meaning of "deer", see note 5 on p. 95. In this context the word will include deer of any species (D.A. 1963 s. 9).

[6] "Night" extends from one hour after sunset to one hour before sunrise (D.A. 1963 s. 2).

[7] D.A. 1963 ss. 2, 4 (1).

[8] D.A. 1963 ss. 10 (1) (2), 11 (1).

[9] D.A. 1963 s. 4 (1).

calculated to cause bodily injury to any deer coming into contact with it.[1]

(2) Using, for the purpose of killing any deer, —

    *(a) any smooth bore gun or any cartridge for use in it,

    (b) any rifle of a calibre less than 0.240 inches or a muzzle energy of less than 1,700 foot pounds,

    (c) any bullet for use in a rifle, other than a soft-nosed or hollow-nosed bullet,

    (d) any air gun, air rifle, or air pistol,[2]

    (e) any missile, whether discharged from a firearm[3] or otherwise, carrying or containing any poison, stupefying drug or muscle-relaxing agent.[4]

*(3) Discharging any firearm[3] or projecting any missile from any mechanically propelled vehicle or aircraft at any deer.[5]

*(4) Using any mechanically propelled vehicle or aircraft for the purpose of driving deer.[6]

(5) Possessing,[7] for the purpose of committing any other offence under the 1963 Deer Act, any fire-

---

[1] D.A. 1963 s. 3 (1) (b).

[2] The descriptions of guns and ammunition in sub-paras. (a)–(d) may be varied by order of the Home Office (D.A. 1963 s. 3 (4)).

[3] The definition of "firearm" examined in Chapter 1 applies (D.A. 1963 s. 9; F.A. 1968 s. 57 (1)).

[4] D.A. 1963 s. 3 (1) (c), Sch. 2.

[5] D.A. 1963 ss. 3 (2) (a), 9.

[6] D.A. 1963 ss. 3 (2) (b), 9.

[7] For some notes on the meaning of "possession", *see* pp. 20–22.

arm[1] or ammunition[2] or any weapon or article which is described at items (1) or (2) above.[3]

The defences which are available in some instances are:

(A) In the case of the offence at (2) (a) above, that the gun was used[4] for the purpose of killing a deer if the user can show[5] that it had been so seriously injured, otherwise than by his unlawful act,[6] or was in such a condition, that to kill it was an act of mercy.[7]

(B) In the case of the offence at (2) (a) above, that the gun was used as a slaughtering instrument[8] to kill deer, provided the gun—

    (i) was of not less gauge than 12 bore, **and**

    (ii) had a barrel less than 24 inches (609.6 mm) in length, **and**

    (iii) was loaded with a cartridge purporting to contain shot none of which was less than 0.203 inches (5.16 mm) in diameter (size AAA or larger).[9]

(C) In the case of the offence at (2) (a) above, that a gun of not less gauge than 12 bore was used by an

---

[1] The definition of "firearm" examined in Chapter 1 applies (D.A. 1963 s. 9; F.A. 1968 s. 57 (1)).

[2] For the definition of "ammunition" which applies, *see* pp. 8–9 (D.A. 1963 s. 9; F.A. 1968 s. 57 (2) (4)).

[3] D.A. 1963 ss. 3 (1) (b) (c), 4 (2), 9. To secure a conviction for this offence, it would be necessary for the prosecution to prove to the court's satisfaction a link between possession and the commission, or intended commission, of one of the offences.

[4] The gun, and the ammunition to be used with it, must comply with the requirements at item (B) which follows in the text above; item (A) merely describes the circumstances in which the deer may be shot.

[5] *I.e.*, can convince the court before whom he is prosecuted.

[6] The words "unlawful act" are not restricted to acts made unlawful by the Deer Act of 1963, and will thus, it seems, embrace acts which are otherwise unlawful, *e.g.*, the improper use of a gun without a shot gun certificate.

[7] D.A. 1963 s. 10 (3).

[8] *I.e.*, as the means of killing when justified by the circumstances at item (A) in the text above.

[9] D.A. 1963 s. 10 (4).

authorised person[1] to take or kill deer on any land, and the gun was loaded with—

(i) a cartridge containing a single non-spherical projectile weighing not less than 350 grains (22.68 grammes); **or**

(ii) a cartridge purporting to contain shot each of which was 0.203 inches (5.16 mm) in diameter (Size AAA).[2]

But this defence cannot be relied upon unless the authorised person can show[3] the existence of the three points described in item (i), (ii) and (iii) on page 96.[4]

(D) In the case of the offences at (3) and (4) above, that the prohibited act was done by, or with the written authority of, the occupier of any enclosed land[5] where deer are usually kept and was done in relation to deer on that land.[6]

POWERS OF POLICE AND POWERS OF COURT ON CONVICTION OF OFFENCES

Constables[7] are given wide powers by the 1963 Act. They may without a warrant stop and search suspected persons, search or examine vehicles,[8] weapons, animals and other things for evidence, and seize and detain things which are such evidence and deer, vehicles,[8] animals, weapons and other things which a court may order to be forfeited on conviction.[9]

---

[1] For the meaning of "authorised person", see pp. 95–96.

[2] D.A. 1963 s. 10A (2). Government Ministers may by order alter in any way the types of guns or ammunition in item (C) or apply the provisions in that item to particular areas or to particular species or descriptions of deer (D.A. 1963 s. 10A (4) (6)).

[3] *I.e.*, can convince the court before whom he is prosecuted.

[4] D.A. 1963 s. 10A (3).

[5] No definition is given of "enclosed land", but see p. 70 for a judicial interpretation in another context.

[6] D.A. 1963 s. 3 (3).

[7] For the meaning of "constables", see note 8 on p. 94.

[8] For the meaning of "vehicles", *see* note 2 on p. 93.

[9] D.A. 1963 s.5(1). For police powers of general application, see p. 85.

A constable may enter land[1] (except a dwelling) to exercise the foregoing powers.[2] He may also sell any deer seized, and the net proceeds are to be forfeited in the same manner as the deer sold.[3]

In addition to imposing imprisonment, a fine or both on an offender,[4] a convicting court may order the forfeiture of—

    (a) any deer in respect of which the offence was committed or which was found[5] in the accused's possession; and

    (b) any vehicle,[6] animal, weapon or other thing which—

        (i) was used to commit the offence, or

        (ii) was capable of being used to take, kill or injure deer and was found[5] in the accused's possession.[7]

DEER POACHING

With the purpose of preventing the poaching of deer, the following acts are, subject to the exemptions mentioned below, made offences by the Deer Act of 1980:–

    (1) To enter land[1] in search or pursuit of any deer[8] with the intention of killing or injuring it.[9]

---

[1] "Land" includes buildings and other structures and land covered with water (I.A. 1978 s. 5, Schedule 1).

[2] D.A. 1963 s. 5 (2).

[3] D.A. 1963 s. 5 (3).

[4] For which see note 3 on p. 95.

[5] "Found" presumably refers to things found by a constable and seized or detained by him under the powers described on pp. 100 and 103.

[6] "Vehicle" includes an aircraft, hovercraft or boat (D.A. 1980 ss. 7, 8). For two possible interpretations of "includes", see p. 67 and note 7 thereto.

[7] D.A. 1963 s. 6 (3).

[8] "Deer" in the context of this and the ensuing offences means deer of any species and includes the carcase of any deer or any part of the carcase (D.A. 1980 s. 8).

[9] D.A. 1980 s. 1 (1).

(2) While on any land[1] —

(a) intentionally to kill or injure, or attempt to kill or injure, any deer;

(b) to search for or pursue any deer with the intention of killing or injuring it;

(c) to remove the carcase of any deer.[2]

But these offences are not perpetrated if the person committing the act —

(a) has the consent[3] of the owner or occupier of the land; **or**

(b) has lawful authority[4] to do it;[5] **or**

(c) believes that he would have the consent of the owner or occupier of the land if the owner or occupier knew of his doing the act and the circumstances of it; **or**

(d) believes that he has other lawful authority[6] to do the act.[7]

If an authorised person[8] suspects with reasonable cause that another person is committing or has committed any of these offences on any land, he may require that person to

---

[1] "Land" includes buildings and other structures and land covered with water (I.A. 1978 s. 5, Schedule 1).

[2] D.A. 1980 s. 1 (2).

[3] Although written consent is not required, the possession of it is surer protection.

[4] No definition or explanation of "lawful authority" is given, but these words would cover acts by a tenant of rights to kill or take deer on the land, or by Ministry of Agriculture officers acting under powers given to them to deal with animal diseases.

[5] D.A. 1980 s. 1 (1) (2).

[6] The difference between this defence and that at (b) above is that the former relies only on the defendant's belief that he had lawful authority of some kind other than that described at (c) above. For the belief to be effective as a defence, it is suggested that, though the belief may be mistaken, it must be honestly and reasonably held.

[7] D.A. 1980 s. 1 (3).

[8] "Authorised person" is defined as the owner or occupier of the land or a person authorised by either of them, and includes any person having the right to take or kill deer on the land (D.A. 1980 s. 1 (7)).

give his full name and address and to leave the land at once; failure to do so is an offence.[1]

Constables'[2] powers under the 1980 Act are the same as those given to them by the 1963 Deer Act,[3] but with the addition of venison[4] to the things which may be seized and detained, and venison seized may be sold.[5]

The maximum punishments for offences and the other powers of a convicting court under the 1980 Act are the same as those under the 1963 Act,[6] but additionally in the former case the court may cancel any firearm certificate or shot gun certificate[7] held by the accused.[8]

The 1980 Act also regulates sales of venison and requires licensed game dealers to keep records of their sales of it.[9]

Seals

It is an offence[10] to use, or attempt to use, for the purpose of killing, injuring or taking any seal,[11] any firearm[12] other than a rifle using ammunition[13] having a muzzle energy of not less than 600 footpounds and a bullet weighing not less

---

[1] D.A. 1980 s. 1 (4). This provision does not enable an authorised person to eject the suspected person, but an owner or occupier of the land, or an employee acting under their orders, may eject a trespasser at common law, using only such force as is necessary.

[2] For the meaning of "constables", see note 8 on p. 94.

[3] For which, see pp. 100–101.

[4] "Venison" includes the carcase, or any edible part of the carcase, of a deer (D.A. 1980 s. 8).

[5] D.A. 1980 s. 4.

[6] D.A. 1980 ss. 1 (5) (6), 5 (1) (a) (b). For these punishments and powers, see note 3 on p. 95 and p. 101, respectively.

[7] For these certificates, see, respectively, Chapters 3 and 4.

[8] D.A. 1980 s. 5 (1) (c) (d).

[9] D.A. 1980 ss. 2, 3.

[10] The maximum punishment on summary conviction is a fine at level 4 on the standard scale (currently £1000) (C.S.A. 1970 s. 5 (2)).

[11] Although this means all seals, the grey and common seals are the only species known to inhabit the coasts of Britain.

[12] This word has the same meaning as in the Firearms Act 1968 (C.S.A. 1970 s. 15), as to which *see* pp. 2–8.

[13] This word has the same meaning as in the Firearms Act 1968 (C.S.A. 1970 s. 15), as to which *see* pp. 8–9.

than 45 grains.[1] The following defences will be available in a prosecution for this offence:–

(1) In the case of killing a seal, that it had been so seriously disabled otherwise than by an act of the killer that there was no reasonable chance of its recovering[2];

(2) That the act done was authorised by a licence granted by the Home Office.[3]

(3) That the act was done outside the seaward limits of the territorial waters adjacent to Great Britain.[4,5]

The annual close seasons for seals are as follows:–

Grey seals (*Halichoerus grypus*): 1st September to 31st December

Common seals (*Phoca vitulina*): 1st June to 31st August[6]

It is an offence[7] wilfully[8] to kill or injure, or attempt to kill or injure, these seals during their close seasons.[9] The same acts are also offences[7] if done at any time of the year in an area designated for the conservation of seals by an order made by the Home Office.[10] Two such orders have been made: one relates to common seals and the other to grey seals. Both orders are in force up to an including 18th. December 1990 unless previously revoked.

The first order affects common seals in Great Britain[5] and

---

[1] C.S.A.1970 ss. 1 (1), 8 (1). The descriptions given of firearms and ammunition may be altered by order of the Home Office (C.S.A. 1970 s. 1 (2)).

[2] C.S.A. 1970 ss. 1 (1), 9 (2).

[3] C.S.A. 1970 ss. 1 (1), 10. For further details of such a licence, *see* pp. 105–106.

[4] C.S.A. 1970 s. 17 (2). The breadth of territorial waters adjacent to Great Britain is 12 nautical miles (1 nautical mile = 1852 metres). The baselines from which this measurement is taken are to be laid down by Orders in Council from time to time (T.S.A. 1987 s.1).

[5] For the meaning of "Great Britain", *see* note 7 on p. 27.

[6] C.S.A. 1970 s. 2 (1). All dates are inclusive.

[7] For penalty, *see* note 10 on p. 103.

[8] This means deliberately and intentionally, and not by accident or inadvertence (*R. v. Senior* [1899] 1 Q.B. 283 at pp. 290–91).

[9] C.S.A. 1970 ss. 2 (2), 8 (1).

[10] C.S.A. 1970 ss. 3.8(1).

within the seaward limits of the adjacent territorial waters.[1]
The second order affects grey seals in England and Wales
and within the seaward limits of the adjacent territorial
waters.[2]

The following defences are available to an accused for
either a close season offence or an offence under the terms
of the two orders: —

(i) That the killing or injuring of the seal was unavoidable and the incidental result of a lawful action.[3]

(ii) That the killing or attempted killing of any seal was
to prevent it from causing damage to a fishing net
or fishing tackle in the accused's possession or in
the possession of a person at whose request he
killed or attempted to kill the seal, or to any fish
for the time being in such fishing net, provided that
at the time[4] the seal was in the vicinity of such net
or tackle;[5]

(iii) The defences described in items (1), (2) and (3) on
page 104.[6]

The Home Office[7] may grant a licence to any person
to kill or take seals and, provided this is done within the

---

[1] Conservation of Seals (Common Seals) Order 1988. As to territorial waters,
see note 4 on p. 104.

[2] Conservation of Seals (England and Wales) Order 1988. In this case the
territorial waters are defined by the Order to mean –
(a) on the east coast, the territorial waters south of a line drawn at 055° true
from the point on the mainland at 55° 48'.67 North latitude and 02° 02'.0
West longitude; and
(b) on the west coast, the territorial waters south of a line drawn at 050° true
from Point of Ayre light on the Isle of Man to the Barnkirk Point light near
Annan: provided that any waters which are nearer to any point on the coast
of Scotland than to any point on the coasts of England or Northern Ireland
shall be deemed to be north of that line.

[3] C.S.A. 1970 ss. 2(2), 3(2), 9(1)(b).

[4] *I.e.*, at the time of killing or attempted killing.

[5] C.S.A. 1970 ss. 2 (2), 3 (2), 9 (1) (c).

[6] C.S.A. 1970 ss. 2 (2), 3 (2), 9 (2), 10, 17 (2). A further defence is available
to a person who takes or attempts to take a seal, which had been disabled otherwise
than by his act, if it was taken or to be taken solely for the purpose of tending it
and releasing it when no longer disabled (C.S.A. 1970 ss. 2 (2), 3 (2), 9 (1) (a)).

[7] Requests for application forms for a licence should be addressed to the Home
Office. H3 Division, Queen Anne's Gate, London SW1H 9AT.

terms and conditions of the licence, no offence will be committed. The purposes for which a licence may be given are:–

(a) For scientific or educational purposes;

(b) For preventing damage to fisheries, for preventing a population surplus of seals for management purposes, or for using a population surplus of seals as a resource.

In all cases the licence will authorise a killing or taking in the area described in the licence which will also specify the means to be used and the number of seals to be killed or taken.[1] The licence may be revoked at any time by the Home Office.[2] A person who contravenes, attempts to contravene, or fails to comply with, any condition of the licence commits an offence.[3]

Any person who, for the purpose of committing any of the offences described,[4] has in his possession,[5] or attempts to have in his possession, any poisonous substance or any prohibited firearm or ammunition[6] commits an offence.[7]

A court convicting a person of any of the offences described[8] may order the forfeiture of any seal or seal skin in respect of which the offence was committed, or any seal,

---

[1] C.S.A. 1970 s. 10 (1). The use of strychnine cannot be authorised by a licence. The taking of seals for a zoological garden or a collection may also be covered by a licence.

[2] No reasons for revocation are laid down, thus giving the Home Office a free hand in this respect. Before granting a licence the Home Office must consult the Nature Conservancy Council (C.S.A. 1970 s. 10 (3)).

[3] C.S.A. 1970 ss. 8 (1), 10 (2). For the maximum punishment, see note 10 on p. 103. Prosecution for this offence will not affect liability for another penalty under this or any other Act.

[4] And also the offences of obstructing or attempting to obstruct the entry on land or water of a person authorised in writing to enter by the Minister of Agriculture (C.S.A. 1970 s. 8 (1), 11 (7)).

[5] For some guidance on the meaning of "possession", see pp. 20–22.

[6] I.e., any firearm or ammunition other than the types described on pp. 103–104.

[7] C.S.A. 1970 ss. 1 (1) (b), 8. For the maximum punishment, see note 10 on p. 103. For commentary on a similar offence in another context, see p. 94.

[8] Including those mentioned in note 4 above.

seal skin, firearm, ammunition or poisonous substance in his possession[1] at the time of the offence.[2]

Constables[3] are given wide powers to enforce the Act. They may stop any person suspected by them with reasonable cause of committing any of the offences described and may—

(1) Without warrant search any vehicle or boat which that person may be using at the time he is stopped by the constable; and

(2) Seize any seal, seal skin, firearm, ammunition or poisonous substance which is liable to be forfeited by order of a court as described above.[4]

A constable[3] may also sell or otherwise dispose of any seal seized in this way, and the net proceeds of sale are liable to forfeiture in the same manner as the seal sold.[5]

Badgers

It is an offence[6] wilfully[7] to kill or injure, or to attempt to kill or injure, any badger.[8] If, in a prosecution for attempt, there is evidence from which it could be reasonably concluded that at the material time the accused was attempting to kill or injure, he shall be presumed to have been so attempting.[9] A number of defences is available and these, so far as shooting is concerned, are—

(1) In the case of a killing or attempted killing, or in the case of injuring a badger in the course of

---

[1] For some guidance on the meaning of "possession", see pp. 20–22.

[2] C.S.A. 1970 s. 6.

[3] For the meaning of "constables", see note 8 on p. 94.

[4] C.S.A. 1970 s. 4 (1).

[5] C.S.A. 1970 s. 4 (2). For police powers of general application, see p. 85

[6] The maximum punishment on summary conviction is a fine at level 5 on the standard scale (currently £2000) for each badger against which the offence is committed. (B.A. 1973 s. 10 (2) (*b*) and proviso.)

[7] This means deliberately and intentionally, and not by accident or inadvertence. (*R. v. Senior* [1899] 1 Q.B. 283 at 290–91).

[8] B.A. 1973 s. 1 (1). "Badger" means any animal of the species *Meles meles* (B.A. 1973 s. 11).

[9] B.A. 1973 s. 1(1A); W.C. (A)A. 1985 s. 1(1).

attempting to kill it, that the defendant can show[1] that his action was necessary for the purpose of preventing serious damage to land,[2] crops, poultry or any other form of property; **but** this defence is **not** available in relation to any action taken at any time if it had become apparent, before that time, that that action would prove necessary for the purpose mentioned, **and**

either (a) a licence authorising that action had not been applied for as soon as reasonably practicable after the fact of the action proving necessary had become apparent;

or (b) an application for such a licence had been determined.[3]

(2) That it was a killing or attempted killing of a badger which appeared to be so seriously injured or in such a condition that to kill it would be an act of mercy.[4]

(3) That it was an unavoidable killing or injuring as an incidental result of a lawful action.[5]

(4) That the act was done under the authority of, and within the conditions of, a licence, the provisions for which are next considered.[6]

Licences related to shooting may be granted for the following purposes:–

(i) For scientific or educational purposes, to kill within the area and by the means described in the licence, or to sell or have in the licensed persons' possession the number of badgers stipulated by the licence;

(ii) For the purpose of preventing the spread of dis-

---

[1] *I.e.*, can satisfy the court before whom he is prosecuted.

[2] "Land" is defined to include, amongst other things, buildings and other structures and land covered with water (I.A. 1978 s. 5, Schedule 1).

[3] B.A. 1973 s. 8 (1A), (1B). For comment on the same defence in another context, see note 9 on p. 90.

[4] B.A. 1973 s. 8 (1) (b).

[5] B.A. 1973 s. 8 (1) (c). An example of this defence would be an accident between a vehicle and a badger on a road.

[6] B.A. 1973 s. 9 (1).

ease, to kill badgers within the area and by the means described in the licence;

(iii) For the purpose of preventing serious damage to land,[1] crops, poultry or any other form of property, to kill badgers within the area and by the means described in the licence.[2]

In the first case licences are granted by the Nature Conservancy Council[3] and in the last two cases by the Minister of Agriculture or, in Scotland, the Secretary of State for Scotland.[4] A licence may be revoked at any time,[5] and breach of its conditions is an offence.[6]

The 1973 Act creates a number of other offences related to badgers, some with special defences, and these will now be considered.

Unless permitted by or under the 1973 Act,[7] it is an offence[8] for any person to have in his possession[9] or under his control any dead badger or any part of, or anything derived from, a dead badger.[10] But it is a defence if the person shows that[11] —

(a) the badger had not been killed;[12] **or**

---

[1] For the definition of "land", see note 2 on p. 108.

[2] B.A. 1973 s. 9 (1).

[3] Application should be made to the Council at 19–20 Belgrave Square, London S.W.1.

[4] B.A. 1973 s. 9 (2). Applications to the Minister should be made to the Divisional Executive Officer at the Ministry's local Divisional Office. In Scotland applications should be sent to the Divisional Veterinary Officer at the local Animal Health Office.

[5] No reasons for revocation are laid down, thus giving to the licensing authorities a free hand in this respect, as indeed they have in deciding whether to issue a licence in the first place.

[6] B.A. 1973 s. 9 (3). For the maximum punishment, see note 6 on p. 107.

[7] E.g., under the terms of a licence.

[8] For the maximum punishment, see note 6 on p. 107.

[9] For some notes on the meaning of "possession", see pp. 20–22.

[10] B.A. 1973 s. 1 (2).

[11] I.e., can convince the court before which he is prosecuted.

[12] This seems to be a piece of loose terminology prompting the question: killed by whom or what? The words are perhaps intended to cover the case of a badger dying of natural causes, though the need for distinguishing between that event and death by accident is unclear.

(b) it had been killed otherwise than in contravention of the Act; **or**

(c) the object in the persons's possession or control had been sold (whether to him or any other person) **and**, at the time of purchase, the purchaser had had no reason to believe that the badger had been killed in contravention of the Act.[1]

Described as offences of cruelty,[2] the following acts are forbidden:–

(a) cruelly to ill-treat any badger;

(b) to use any badger tongs in the course of killing, or attempting to kill, any badger;

(c) to use, for the purpose of killing or taking any badger, any firearm[3] other than a smooth bore weapon of not less than 20 bore or a rifle using ammunition[3] having a muzzle energy of not less than 160 foot pounds and a bullet weighing not less than 38 grains.[4]

Constables[5] are given wide powers to enforce the 1973 Act. If a constable has reasonable grounds for suspecting that any person is committing or had committed an offence under the Act **and** that evidence of the commission of the offence is to be found on that person or any vehicle or article he may have with him,[6] he may—

(1) without a warrant stop and search that person and search any vehicle or article he may have with him;[6] **and**

(2) seize and detain for the purposes of a prosecution under the Act anything which may be evidence of

---

[1] B.A. 1973 s. 1 (3).

[2] For the maximum punishment, see note 6 on p. 107

[3] The definitions of these words in the Firearms Act 1968 are applied. (B.A. 1973 s. 11). For a discussion of them, *see* pp. 2–9.

[4] B.A. 1973 s. 2. Digging for badgers is also forbidden unless permitted by or under the 1973 Act, *e.g.*, by a licence (B.A. 1973 s. 2 (c)).

[5] For the meaning of this word, *see* note 8 on p. 94.

[6] For an interpretation of the words "have with him", *see* p. 128.

the commission of the offence or may be liable to be forfeited by a convicting court.[1]

On conviction of any offence under the Act the court **must** order forfeiture of any badger or badger's skin in respect of which the offence was committed, and **may** order forfeiture of weapons and articles connected with the offence.[2]

If any person is found on land committing any of the offences described on page 107 or having illegal possession of a dead badger or things derived from it,[3] the owner or occupier of the land, or an employee of either, or a constable,[4] may require that person to leave the land at once and give his name and address. If the person then deliberately remains on the land or refuses to give his particulars, he commits an offence.[5]

Other Wild Creatures

Wild creatures other than those described in the previous Sections of this Chapter are protected only in the sense that there is a substantial body of law designed to prevent cruelty and unnecessary suffering, and this mainly affects domestic animals. Such law, not being directly concerned with the use of guns, is not within the scope of this book.

Finally, it should be known that it is an offence to destroy or damage[6] wild creatures no longer in a wild state[7] "without lawful excuse" — an expression lengthily defined.[8]

---

[1] B.A. 1973 s. 10 (1). For police power of general application, see p. 85

[2] B.A. 1973 s. 10 (3).

[3] For such illegal possession, *see* p. 109–110.

[4] For the meaning of this word, see note 8 on p. 94.

[5] B.A. 1973 s. 5. The maximum punishment on summary conviction for this offence is a fine at level 3 on the standard scale (currently £400). (B.A. 1973 s. 10 (2) (*a*).)
Note that this provision gives no right to the persons named forcibly to eject the offender from the land. If he is a trespasser, the common law powers of ejectment summarised on p. 80 will apply.

[6] The word "damage" is used because the Act of Parliament creating the offence is primarily concerned with damage to lifeless property.

[7] *I.e.*, tamed, ordinarily kept in captivity or otherwise reduced or being reduced into possession.

[8] C.D.A. 1971 ss. 1 (1) (2), 5, 10 (1) (*a*).

CHAPTER 13

THE TENANT'S RIGHT TO SHOOT

The general, or Common Law, rule is that the right to possession of land carries with it the right to take all birds and animals naturally on the land, whether they be game or not.[1] Thus, if you have a tenancy of land, unless the shooting is "reserved" to the landlord in your tenancy agreement, you will have an absolute right to shoot as against any other person. Conversely, if the right to take game is "reserved", you have no right[2] to shoot at Common Law.[3] This is expressly stated in the Game Act of 1831,[4] and an offence is created by Section 12 of that Act.[5] Similarly, an owner of land, whether in occupation of it or not, has no right at Common Law[6] to shoot over it if he has let the shooting. An occupier with full shooting rights may authorise any person to kill and take game and other birds and animals, and the authority need not be in writing; he may also let or assign his shooting rights.

The position at Common Law was much altered by the Ground Game Act which was passed in 1880. The Act, the object of which was to allow tenants not having shooting rights to protect their crops against hares and rabbits, permits occupiers of land to kill and take ground game[7] on

---

[1] Rare exceptions to this rule apply where sporting rights are given to lords of manors under Inclosure Acts and Awards.

[2] Although, of course, the landlord may permit you to shoot.

[3] You will, however, have a statutory right to shoot hares and rabbits under the provisions of the Ground Game Acts about to be considered which make void any "reservation" of these animals to the landlord (G.G.A. 1880 s. 3).

[4] G.A. 1831, s. 8, which also forbids the occupier to permit another person to shoot.

[5] For details of the offence, see p. 116.

[6] But, if in occupation, will have a statutory right to shoot hares and rabbits.

[7] "Ground Game" is the term in the Act used to describe hares and rabbits (G.G.A. 1880 s. 8).

112

their land concurrently with any other person who may have the right to do the same thing.[1] Within certain limitations, tenants may also claim compensation from their landlords for damage to crops caused by any wild animals or birds.[2]

There are some extensions to, and several limitations on, this right of the occupier to take ground game, and these will now be considered.

First, who is an occupier? Clearly, an occupying owner, tenant or sub-tenant of land will be. The Act says that a person having a right of common or "an occupation for the purpose of grazing or pasturage of sheep, cattle, or horses for not more than nine months" will not be an occupier.[3] It would seem to follow from this that if the occupation for the purposes quoted exceeds nine months, the occupier will be qualified under the Act, but this has been questioned and the contrary view put that the occupier must have the right to full possession of the land and not a limited right to its use, as in the case of a licensee.[4] Doubts also arise in cases where land is used for grazing other animals such as goats and pigs. Where there are joint occupiers all are entitled to the rights conferred by the Act.[5]

In addition to the occupier, one other person authorised by the occupier in writing[6] may shoot[7] ground game.[8] This person can only be:–

---

[1] G.G.A. 1880 s. 1.
[2] A.H.A. 1986 s. 20.
[3] G.G.A. 1880 s. 1 (2).
[4] *See Oke's Game Laws*, 5th Edition, p. 103.
[5] *Oke's Game Laws*, 5th Edition, pp. 101–2.
[6] The authority need not be in any prescribed form, but it should be legibly signed and dated, describe the person to whom it is given and precisely state the situation and extent of the land over which it is to operate.
[7] More than one person may, however, be authorised to take ground game otherwise than by using firearms.
[8] G.G.A. 1880 s. 1 (1) (*a*). Where there are joint occupiers, it seems that all must give their authority to one other person to shoot and that each cannot authorise a different person (*Oke's Game Laws*, 5th Edition, p. 102).

(1) A member of the occupier's household[1] resident[2] on the land in his occupation, the shooting authority extending only to that land; or

(2) A person in the occupier's ordinary service[3] on the land occupied, the shooting authority extending only to that land; or

(3) Any one other person *bona fide* employed by the occupier for reward[4] in the taking and destruction of ground game.[5]

More than one person from classes (1) and (2) above, but only one from class (3), may, at the same time, kill and take ground game otherwise than by shooting if, again, they are authorised in writing by the occupier.[5]

An authorised person must produce his written authority, if asked to do so, to any person having a concurrent right to take or kill ground game on the land or to any person authorised by the latter in writing to make the demand. In default, the authorised person's rights cease.[6]

In the case of moorlands and unenclosed non-arable land, except detached portions of either which are less than 25 acres in extent and adjoin arable lands, the time at which the right of the occupier may be exercised is limited. Between 11th December of one year and 31st March (both inclusive) of the following year the right may be exercised and ground game may be killed in any legal way by the occupier and persons authorised by him in accordance with

---

[1] This will include servants who live and board at the house, but not those living in other houses on the farm (*Re Drax, Savile v. Yeatman* (1887) 57 L.T. 475; *Ogle v. Morgan* (1852) 1 De G.M. & G. 359).

[2] This will include a visitor staying at the house but presumably not one who comes for a day.

[3] "Ordinary service" may include labour regularly employed but for a certain season only.

[4] The fact of, for example, a rabbit-catcher being allowed to keep all or some of the rabbits taken would probably be sufficient evidence of such employment for reward (*Bruce v. Prosser* (1898) 35 Sc. L.R. 433), but a similar gift to a friend asked to come and shoot would hardly be so.

[5] G.G.A. 1880 s. 1 (1) (*b*).

[6] G.G.A. 1880 s. 1 (1) (*c*).

the Act.[1] Between 1st April and 31st August (both inclusive) the right is suspended altogether. Between 1st September and 10th December (both inclusive) the right may be exercised otherwise than by the use of firearms.[2]

The occupier of land, **or** one other person[3] authorised by him, may now[4] use firearms[5] to kill hares and rabbits at night[6] on that land if—

(a) the occupier has the exclusive right to kill and take hares and rabbits on the land; **or**

(b) the occupier has the written authority[7] of the other person, or one of the other persons,[8] who has that right.[9]

The Act is at pains to ensure that an occupier retains the shooting rights which it gives to him. Thus, if an occupier has the right to shoot hares and rabbits otherwise than by the powers given to him by the Act and he transfers that right to another person, he nevertheless keeps his statutory shooting rights.[10] Again, any agreement, condition or arrangement which tries to divest the occupier of his rights

---

[1] G.G.A. 1880 s. 1 (3).

[2] G.G.A. 1906 s. 2. This Act refers to the occupier only, whereas G.G.A. 1880 s. 1 (3) also mentions persons authorised by him. Thus, it seems, only the occupier himself may take ground game, otherwise than by shooting, between 1st September and 10th December. The occupier may make an agreement with the owner of, or any other person having the right to take game on, lands of this description, for the joint exercise, or the exercise for their joint benefit, of the right to kill and take ground game within this period of the year (G.G.A. 1906 s. 3).

[3] Who must be a person within one of the descriptions given in items (1)–(3) on p. 114. As to the form of authority, see the suggestions in note 6 on p. 113.

[4] Since 16th February 1982. Previously, what is now permitted was, for occupying tenants, an offence.

[5] The definition of "firearm" discussed at pp. 2–8 applies (F.A. 1968 s. 57 (1); W.C.A. 1981 ss. 12, 27 (1), Schedule 7, para. 1 (1)).

[6] From one hour after sunset to hour before sunrise (W.C.A. 1981, s. 12, Schedule 7, para. 1 (1)).

[7] Impliedly, this will be an authority to the occupier to use firearms at night for the purpose described, which need not, it is suggested, embrace others whom the occupier himself may authorise under this provision.

[8] As to who these persons may be, see p. 112.

[9] W.C.A. 1981 s. 12, Schedule 7, para. 1.

[10] G.G.A. 1880 s. 2. This means that both persons have concurrent rights to shoot hares and rabbits.

under the Act, or which gives him an advantage in return for his forbearing to exercise those rights, is declared to be void.[1] As the Act twice declares,[2] the rights which it gives to the occupier are "incident (*sic*) to and inseparable from" his occupation of the land.

On the other hand, nothing in the Act is to restrict the occupier's shooting rights to those rights which it gives to him, and he may acquire in the usual way, and exercise, the right to shoot ground game and other game.[3]

Where the occupier has no shooting rights, except those given to him by the Act, and he shoots game,[4] other than hares and rabbits, or gives permission to any other person to do so, without in either case the authority of the person who has the right of killing that game, he commits an offence.[5]

---

[1] G.G.A. 1880 s. 3.

[2] G.G.A. 1880 ss. 1 and 2.

[3] G.G.A. 1880 s. 2. This means, for example, that an occupying tenant, whose lease does not reserve shooting rights to his landlord, may shoot ground game with freedom from the restrictions which the Act would impose if his right to shoot rested solely on the provisions of the Act.

[4] Game in this context includes hares, pheasants, partridges, grouse, heath or moor game and black game (G.A. 1831 s. 2). As to "includes", see text and note 7 on p. 67.

[5] G.A. 1831 s. 12. The maximum punishment on summary conviction is a fine at level 1 on the standard scale (currently £50) plus a similar fine for each head of game so taken.

CHAPTER 14

YOUNG PEOPLE AND GUNS

To all the other regulations and restrictions affecting the use of guns and their ammunition Parliament has added special provisions for young people under 17 years of age.[1] These provisions vary according to age, depending upon whether the person is under 14, under 15 or under 17, vary again according to the kind of act done in relation to firearms and ammunition, and vary yet again according to the type of firearm or ammunition which is involved. A number of offences is created, many of them with exceptions. This produces a complex situation which may perhaps best be examined by considering each of the offences in turn and seeing how each applies to the different age groups and what exceptions each may have. For further clarity, a table is given at pages 124 and 125 of this Chapter dealing with all these elements in summary form.

The general exceptions to firearms' law in the cases of proof houses and antique firearms, which are considered at the end of Chapter 1, apply to young people as to others. It must also be borne in mind that the possession of and other dealings with firearms by young people which are permitted under the headings now to be discussed will nevertheless in many cases be illegal unless covered by the necessary firearm or shot gun certificate the need for which is discussed in Chapters 3 and 4.

---

[1] A person attains a particular age expressed in years at the beginning of the relevant anniversary of the date of his birth (F.L.R.A. 1969 s. 9 (1)). Thus, a person becomes 17 at the midnight immediately preceding his 17th birthday.

It is, perhaps, curious that no minimum age is stipulated.

117

A. Firearms and Ammunition

Both these words are given lengthy definitions in the Firearms Act of 1968 which are fully discussed in Chapter 1.[1] These definitions catch all ordinary kinds of firearms and ammunition and, in the case of firearms, component parts and accessories for reducing noise or flash are included. Imitation firearms fulfilling the conditions described on pages 62–63 will also be subject to the following rules.

BUYING OR HIRING

No person under 17 may buy or hire **any** firearm or ammunition.[2] It is also an offence for any person to sell[3] or let on hire any firearm or ammunition to a youngster under 17 unless he can prove that he believed the youngster to be of or over that age and had reasonable ground for the belief.[4]

POSSESSING

Youngsters aged 14 or over may have Section 1 firearms or Section 1 ammunition[5] in their possession[6]. Those under 14 can only do so in the following situations[7]:–

    (1) Whilst carrying firearms or ammunition belonging to a person holding a firearm certificate or shot gun certificate, the carrying being under instructions from, and for the use of, that person for sporting purposes only;[8]

---

[1] *See* pp. 2–8 as to firearms and pp. 8–9 as to ammunition.

[2] F.A. 1968 s. 22 (1). The maximum punishment on summary conviction is 6 months' imprisonment, or a fine at level 5 on the standard scale (currently £2000), or both (F.A. 1968 s. 51 (1), (2) and Schedule 6, Part I).

[3] A sale, a condition of which is that the seller retains possession of the firearm and where the seller in fact retains subsequent physical possession, allowing the buyer only to have it to use at a rifle club, is nevertheless a sale for the purpose of this offence (*Watts v. Seymour* [1967] 1 All E.R. 1044).

[4] F.A. 1968 s. 24 (1), (5). For maximum punishment, *see* note[2] above.

[5] For the meanings of "Section 1 firearm" and "Section 1 ammunition", see pp. 18–20.

[6] For commentary on the meaning of "possession", *see* pp. 20–22.

[7] Otherwise an offence is committed; for maximum punishment, *see* note 2 above.

[8] F.A. 1968 ss. 11 (1), 22 (2). The shooting of rats is not shooting for sporting purposes only (*Morton v. Chaney* [1960] 3 All E.R. 632).

(2) As a member of an approved rifle club, miniature rifle club, pistol club or cadet corps[1] whilst engaged as such a member in, or in connection with, drill or target practice;[2]

(3) For conducting or carrying on a miniature rifle range (whether for a rifle club or otherwise) or shooting gallery at which, in either case, no fire-arms are used other than air weapons[3] or miniature rifles not exceeding .23 inch calibre, a person under 14 may have in his possession[4] such miniature rifles and ammunition suitable for them[5].

It is an offence for a person to part with the possession of Section 1 firearms or Section 1 ammunition[6] to any child under the age of 14, except in those cases where the under–14 is allowed to have possession as described above.[7] It will be a defence for the accused person to prove that he believed the child to be aged at least 14 and had reasonable ground for the belief.[8]

GIFTS AND LOANS

A person may not make a gift of or lend Section 1 firearms or Section 1 ammunition[6] to a youngster aged under 14. To do so is an offence[9] unless the person accused can prove that he believed the youngster to be 14 or over and had reasonable ground for that belief.[8]

---

[1] As to the approval of rifle and pistol clubs and cadet corps, see pp. 24–25.

[2] F.A. 1968 ss. 11 (3), 22 (2); F.(A)A. 1988 ss. 15, 23 (4).

[3] This means an air gun, air rifle or air pistol, not being of a type declared by rules made by the Home Office to be specially dangerous (F.A. 1968 ss. 1 (3) (b), 57 (4)). For rules so made, see p. 18.

[4] It seems that the youngster may use the ammunition and rifles in addition to simply handling them.

[5] F.A. 1968 ss. 1(3),(3A), 11(1),(3),(4), 22(2); F.(A)A. 1988 ss. 2, 15, 23(4).

[6] For the meanings of "Section 1 firearm" and "Section 1 ammunition", see pp. 18–20.

[7] F.A. 1968 ss. 1 (3), (3A), (4), 11 (1), (3), (4), 24 (2) (b); F.(A)A. 1988 ss. 2, 15, 23 (4). For maximum punishment, see note 2 on p. 118.

[8] F.A. 1968 s. 24 (5).

[9] F.A. 1968 ss. 1 (3), (3A), (4), 24 (2) (a); F.(A)A. 1988 s. 2. For maximum punishment, see note 2 on p. 118.

It is no longer expressly made an offence for a child under 14 to accept a gift or loan in a case where the donor or lender commits an offence, though, technically, if the child assists the offender, the child is guilty as an accessory to the offence.

B. Shot Guns and Shot Gun Ammunition

The definition of "shot gun" is given on pages 41 and 42. There is no statutory definition of "shot gun ammunition".

GIFTS

A person may make a gift of a shot gun or shot gun ammunition to a youngster aged 15 or over, but not to one aged under 15.[1] Again, it is a defence if the accused person can prove that he believed the youngster to be 15 or over and had reasonable ground for that belief.[2]

HAVING AN ASSEMBLED SHOT GUN

A child aged less than 15 must not have an assembled shot gun with him[3] except while under the supervision of a person at least 21 years old or while the gun is so covered with a securely fastened gun cover that it cannot be fired.[4] Youngsters of 15 and over may have assembled shot guns with them without either of these restrictions.

C. Air Weapons and Air Weapon Ammunition

The following rules about young persons having air weapons and ammunition with them and about gifts of these to them relate only to air weapons not declared to be specially

---

[1] F.A. 1968 ss. 1, 24(3); F.(A)A. 1988 s. 2. The maximum punishment on summary conviction is a fine at level 3 on the standard scale (currently £400) (F.A. 1968 s. 51 (1), (2) and Schedule 6, Part I).

[2] F.A. 1968 s. 24 (5).

[3] It seems that the words "with him" will cover the case of a gun being on or in a vehicle carrying a youngster. He will only be liable for conviction if he knew that the gun was with him (*R. v. Cugullere* [1961] 2 All E.R. 343). *See also* p. 128.

[4] F.A. 1968 ss. 1, 22(3); F.(A)A. 1988 s. 2. For maximum punishment, *see* note 1 above.

dangerous[1] and to air weapon ammunition generally.[2] If they are specially dangerous, they fall into the same category, for the purposes of this Chapter, as Section 1 firearms and must be considered under Head A. above.

In the following paragraphs "air weapon" means an air rifle, air gun or air pistol.[3]

HAVING AN AIR WEAPON IN A PUBLIC PLACE AND ELSEWHERE

No person under 17 shall have an air weapon with him[4] in a public place[5] except an air gun or air rifle[6] which is so covered with a securely fastened gun cover that it cannot be fired.[7] To this rule there are two further exceptions, as follows:–

(1) If the youngster is engaged as a member of a rifle club or miniature rifle club in, or in connection with, target practice, and that club is approved by the Home Office.[8]

(2) If the youngster is using the air weapon at a shooting gallery where the only firearms used are either air weapons which are not specially dangerous or miniature rifles not exceeding .23 inches in calibre.[9]

A child aged under 14 must not have with him[4] **in any place** an air weapon or ammunition for an air weapon, but the child commits no offence whilst in any one of the following situations:–

(i) While under the supervision of a person aged at least 21; but if, in these circumstances, he fires a

---

[1] For details, see p. 18.

[2] F.A. 1968 ss. 22 (4), (5), 23, 24 (4), 57 (4).

[3] F.A. 1968 ss. 1 (3) (*b*), 57 (4).

[4] For the meaning of "have with him", *see* note 3 on p. 120.

[5] For the meaning of "public place", *see* p. 128. It has been decided that a piece of field surrounded by boundary fences and separated from the highway in which a number of boys were "larking about" (though whether they had permission is not recorded) was not a public place (*Gorely v. Codd* [1966] 3 All E.R. 891).

[6] But not, it should be noted, an air pistol.

[7] F.A. 1968 s. 22 (5). For maximum punishment, *see* note 1 on p. 120.

[8] As to approval of rifle clubs by the Home Office, *see* note 3 on p. 24.

[9] F.A. 1968 s. 23 (2); F.(A)A. 1988 ss. 15, 23(4).

missile from the air weapon beyond the premises[1] where he happens to be, or if the supervisor allows him to do this, an offence is committed.[2]

(ii) While in the situations described in items (1) and (2) on the preceding page.[3]

Youngsters aged 14, 15 and 16 are free to carry air weapons and their ammunition with them unless carrying an air weapon in a public place when the restrictions mentioned above for the under-17s will apply.

PARTING WITH POSSESSION OF AN AIR WEAPON AND ITS AMMUNITION

A person must not part with the possession[4] of an air weapon or air weapon ammunition to a child under 14. But, if he does so in any of the situations described in items (i) and (ii) above, he has a defence.[5] He also has a defence if he can prove that he believed the youngster to be at least 14 and had reasonable ground for that belief.[6]

GIFTS

A person may make a gift of an air weapon or air weapon ammunition to a youngster aged 14 or more, but not if under 14.[7] Again, the person making the gift has a defence if he can prove that he believed the youngster to be at least 14 and had reasonable ground for that belief.[6]

By way of conclusion to this section, it may be helpful to summarise the basic rules about giving and lending air weapons to children under 14, making the distinction between specially dangerous air weapons and those not so classified:

---

[1] The word "premises" is defined as including any land (F.A. 1968 s. 57 (4)).
[2] F.A. 1968 s. 23 (1). For maximum punishment, see note 1 on p. 120.
[3] F.A. 1968 ss. 22 (4), 23. For maximum punishment, see note 1 on p. 120.
[4] For commentary on meaning of the word "possession", see pp. 20–22.
[5] F.A. 1968 ss. 23, 24 (4) (b). For maximum punishment, see note 1 on p. 120.
[6] F.A. 1968 s. 24 (5).
[7] F.A. 1968 s. 24 (4) (a); For maximum punishment, see note 1 on p. 120.

It is an offence to give or lend a specially dangerous air weapon.[1]

It is an offence to give an air weapon which is not specially dangerous.[2]

It is **not** an offence to lend an air weapon which is not specially dangerous.[3]

Upon conviction for an offence mentioned in this Chapter (except an offence relating specifically to air weapons[4] and the offence of having an assembled shot gun[5]) the Court may order the forfeiture or disposal of any firearm or ammunition found in the convicted person's possession,[6] and may cancel that person's firearm certificate or shot gun certificate.[7]

Many of the restrictions discussed above are complicated enough in themselves, but a greater difficulty is caused, when trying to find the answer in any particular case, by the considerable overlapping and duplication of the restrictions. In an attempt to overcome this, there are set out on page 124 in summary form the restricted acts which apply to the different age groups, and on the facing page the exceptions which operate in some cases. The word "Yes" under the "Age" heading indicates that the prohibited act may be done; the word "No" shows that it may not be, except where it is followed by a capital letter referring to an exception, in which case the prohibition is eased to the extent of the exception.

Great care must be taken when using the table. Because of the similarities of some of the expressions and the different descriptions of guns which are used, it is advisable, when considering any particular case, to check the position under each of the prohibited acts.

---

[1] F.A. 1968 ss. 1 (3) (*b*), 24 (2) (*a*).
[2] FA. 1968 ss. 1 (3) (*b*), 24 (4) (*a*), 57 (4).
[3] F.A. 1968 ss. 1 (3) (*b*), 24 (2) (*a*).
[4] For the definition of "air weapons", *see* p. 121.
[5] This offence is described on p. 120.
[6] As to "possession", *see* pp. 20–22.
[7] F.A. 1968 ss. 1 (3) (b), 22 (3), 52 (1), 57 (4).

Restricted Acts	Age		
	Up to and including 13	14	15 to 16 inclusive
I. ACTS BY YOUNGSTERS WHICH ARE PROHIBITED			
1. Buying or hiring any firearm or any ammunition.	No	No	No
2. Having an air weapon[1] with him in a public place.	No A[2], B, C	No A[2], B, C	No A[2], B, C
3. Having an assembled shot gun with him.	No A, D	No A, D	Yes
4. Possessing a Section 1 firearm or ammunition.	*See* pages 118 to 119		
5. Having with him an air weapon[1] or ammunition for an air weapon.	No B, C, D	Yes	Yes
II. ACTS BY OTHERS[3] IN RELATION TO YOUNGSTERS[4]			
6. Selling or letting on hire a Section 1 firearm or ammunition.	No	No	No
7. Giving a shot gun or ammunition for a shot gun.	No	No	Yes
8. Giving a Section 1 firearm or ammunition.	No	Yes	Yes
9. Lending a Section 1 firearm or ammunition.	No	Yes	Yes
10. Parting with possession of a Section 1 firearm or ammunition.	*See* page 119		
11. Giving an air weapon[1] or ammunition for an air weapon.	No	No	Yes
12. Parting with possession of an air weapon[1] or ammunition for an air weapon.	No B, C, D	Yes	Yes

---

[1] The air weapon must not be of a kind declared to be specially dangerous. If of such a kind, the rules relating to Section 1 firearms apply.

[2] Exception A in these instances applies to air guns and air rifles, but not to air pistols.

[3] These may include youngsters as well as adults.

[4] In the case of each of the acts under this heading, it will be a defence for the accused person to prove that he believed the youngster to be of or over the age of 14, 15 or 17 (as the case may be) and that he had reasonable ground for that belief.

Exceptions

A. Gun so covered with a securely fastened gun cover that it cannot be fired.

B. Member of a rifle club or miniature rifle club approved by the Home Office whilst engaged, as a member, in, or in connection with, target practice.

C. Having the weapon or ammunition at a shooting gallery where the only firearms used are air weapons which are not specially dangerous or miniature rifles not exceeding .23 inches calibre.

D. Supervision by a person at least 21 years old.

CHAPTER 15

GENERAL RESTRICTIONS ON SHOOTING AND CARRYING GUNS

Carrying Firearms[1] in Public Places and Buildings and on Land

Any person who without lawful authority or reasonable excuse, the proof whereof shall lie on him, has with him in a public place any loaded shot gun or loaded air weapon or any other firearm (whether loaded or not) together with ammunition suitable for use in that firearm commits an offence.[2] Let us examine the different ingredients of this offence.

"Without lawful authority": these words are not defined in the Act, and there is no certain authority for their interpretation, but it is thought that they are used in the sense of authority supported by law.

"Or reasonable excuse": for there to be a reasonable excuse it must be shown that there was an imminent particular threat affecting the particular circumstances in which the

---

[1] For two general exceptions to the offences considered under this heading, *see* pp. 9–10.

[2] F.A. 1968 s. 19. The maximum punishment on summary conviction is imprisonment for 6 months or the statutory maximum fine (currently £2000) or both; or (unless the firearm is an air weapon) on indictment, 5 years' imprisonment or an unlimited fine or both. (F.A. 1968, s. 51 (1), (2) and Schedule 6, Part I).

weapon was carried. The constant carriage of a weapon on account of some enduring threat or danger, supposed or actual, to the carrier cannot be excused,[1] and neither can the threatening use of a weapon to enforce a private argument.[2] But the carrying of a gun to a rifle range for shooting or the crossing of a public road with a gun during the course of a shoot are, it is suggested, examples of situations in which there was a reasonable excuse.

"The proof whereof shall lie on him": if charged, it will be enough for the defendant to satisfy the Court of the probability of existence of the lawful authority or reasonable excuse.[3]

"Has with him": this should be read as "knowingly has with him".[4] Thus, for example, the person is entitled to be acquitted if he can satisfy the Court that the gun was in the vehicle he was driving without his knowledge. The words have a more restricted meaning than is implied by possession,[5] and extend to any situation where there is a close physical link between the defendant and the gun.[6]

"A public place": this is defined in the Act as including any highway and any other premises or place to which at the material time the public have or are permitted to have access, whether on payment or otherwise.[7] This definition clearly covers places of public entertainment and hotels and public houses during licensing hours and also, it is suggested, buses, trains, aeroplanes and ships running on scheduled services, and taxis whilst available for hire. The space behind the counter in a shop is a public place.[8]

"Loaded": the Act declares that the weapon shall be deemed to be loaded if there is ammunition in the chamber or barrel or in any magazine or other device which is in

[1] *Evans v. Hughes* [1972] 3 All E.R. 412.
[2] *Taylor v. Mucklow* [1973] Crim. L.R. 750.
[3] *R. v. Carre-Briant* [1943] 2 All E.R. 156.
[4] *R. v. Cugullere* [1961] 2 All E.R. 343.
[5] For commentary on the meaning of "possession", *see* pp. 20–22.
[6] *R. v. Kelt* [1977] 1 W.L.R. 1365; Crim. L.R. 556.
[7] F.A. 1968 s. 57 (4).
[8] *Anderson v. Miller and Spearman* [1976] Crim. L.R. 743 D.C.

such a position that the ammunition can be fed into the chamber or barrel by the manual or automatic operation of some part of the weapon.[1]

"Shot gun": the definition is given on pages 41 and 42.

"Air weapon": the Act defines this as an air gun, air rifle or air pistol, not being of a type declared by rules made by the Home Office to be specially dangerous.[2]

"Firearm": the definition discussed on pages 2 to 8 of Chapter 1 applies;[3] briefly, it includes virtually every type of gun, any component part of it and some accessories.

"Ammunition": the definition on pages 8 and 9 of Chapter 1 applies,[3] but the point is that the ammunition is to be suitable for use in the firearm carried at the time.

A general point to be noted in connection with this offence is that a shot gun or air weapon must be loaded for the offence to be committed, but other firearms need not be, provided suitable ammunition is carried.

It is an offence for any person who, while he has a firearm with him[4], enters or is on any land or in any building or part of a building as a trespasser and without reasonable excuse, the proof whereof shall lie on him.[5]

Points arising on the words "firearm", "without reasonable excuse", "the proof whereof shall lie on him" and what is meant by a person having a firearm with him have been discussed above; the following two small matters should be mentioned.

---

[1] F.A. 1968 s. 57 (6) (b).

[2] F.A. 1968 ss. 1 (3) (b), 57 (4). For rules so made, see p. 18.

[3] F.A. 1968 s. 57 (1).

[4] But there will be no offence where there is no evidence that the firearm worked or could be made to work (Grace v. D.P.P. [1989]. Crim. L.R. 365, D.C.; The Times, December 9, 1988)

[5] F.A. 1968 s. 20 (1), (2). If the offence relates to a building, the maximum punishment on summary conviction is imprisonment for six months or the statutory maximum fine (currently £2000), or both; or (unless the firearm is an air weapon), on indictment, 5 years' imprisonment or an unlimited fine or both. If the offence relates to land, the maximum punishment on summary conviction is imprisonment for 3 months or a fine at level 4 on the standard scale (currently £1000), or both (F.A. 1968 s. 51 (1), (2) and Schedule 6, Part I).

"Land", as the Act says,[1] includes "land covered with water", so the mere fact that an offender is afloat will not enable him to escape the penalties of the law.

The word "trespasser" is not defined. As well as having its ordinary meaning, e.g. a person who is on premises without the permission of the occupier of the premises, it includes a person on a public road who is not using it for a legitimate purpose.[2]

Lastly, it should be noted that the police have wide supporting powers in connection with the offences discussed under this head. These include[3] power to require a suspected person to hand over a firearm and ammunition to a constable for examination;[4] power to search a suspected person and to detain him for that purpose; and power to stop and search suspected vehicles.[5]

Having Offensive Weapons in a Public Place

Any person who without lawful authority[6] or reasonable excuse,[6] the proof whereof shall lie on him,[6] has with him[6] in any public place[6] any offensive weapon commits an offence.[7] The term "offensive weapon" is defined as "any article made or adapted for use for causing injury to the

---

[1] F.A. 1968 s. 20 (3).

[2] For ownership of, and rights over, public roads, see pp. 132–133.

[3] The powers specified apply to one or other of the offences but not necessarily to both of them.

[4] Failure to do so is itself an offence carrying a maximum punishment on summary conviction of 3 months' imprisonment, or a fine at level 4 on the standard scale (currently £1000), or both (F.A. 1968 ss. 47 (2), 51 (1), (2) and Schedule 6, Part I).

[5] F.A. 1968 ss. 20, 47 (1), (3)–(6), 50 (2). For police powers of general application, see p. 85.

[6] The different meanings of these ingredients of the offence are discussed on pp. 127–128. The expression "public place" is defined in exactly the same terms as those given on p. 128 (P.C.A. 1953 s. 1 (4)).

[7] P.C.A. 1953 s. 1 (1). The maximum punishments are: on indictment 2 years' imprisonment, or an unlimited fine, or both; on summary conviction, 6 months' imprisonment, or a fine of the prescribed sum (currently £2000), or both (P.C.A. 1953 s. 1 (1); C.L.A. 1977 s. 32 (1)). Upon conviction the court may order the forfeiture or disposal of any weapon in respect of which the offence was committed (P.C.A. 1953 s. 1 (2)).

person or intended by the person having it with him for such use by him".[1]

Clearly, any gun capable of causing injury comes within this definition and so, although the Act was aimed at persons with criminal inclinations, the ordinary citizen must beware lest he commits this offence whilst carrying a gun in a public place; in other words, he should be sure that he has "lawful authority or reasonable excuse".

Trespassing with a Weapon of Offence

A person who is on premises as a trespasser, after having entered as such, is guilty of an offence if, without lawful authority or reasonable excuse, he has with him on the premises any weapon of offence.[2] Several ingredients of this offence require individual examination.

The word "premises" is defined to mean any building, any part of a building under separate occupation, any land ancillary to a building and the site comprising any building or buildings together with any land ancillary to the building or buildings.[3] The word "building" in this definition is itself defined to extend its meaning to any structure other than a movable one, and to any movable structure, vehicle or vessel designed or adapted for use for residential purposes. Part of a building is to be treated as under separate occupation if anyone is in occupation or entitled to occupation of that part as distinct from the whole. Land is to be treated as ancillary to a building if it is adjacent to it and used or intended for use in connection with the occupation of that building or any part of it.[4]

A trespasser is, briefly, a person who is on premises without the permission of the occupier. Additionally, for the purpose of the offence now being considered, a person is

---

[1] P.C.A. 1953 s. 1 (4). For police powers in relation to this offence, see p. 85.
[2] C.L.A. 1977 s. 8 (1). The maximum punishment on summary conviction is a fine at level 5 on the standard scale (currently £2000), or 3 months' imprisonment, or both (C.L.A. 1977 s. 8 (3)).
[3] C.L.A. 1977 s. 12 (1) (a).
[4] C.L.A. 1977 s. 12 (2).

treated as a trespasser if he enters or is on or in occupation of any premises "by virtue of any title derived from a trespasser or any licence or consent given by a trespasser or by a person deriving title from a trepasser."[1] The effect of the legal phraseology quoted here is that a person who is on premises by some arrangement with a trespasser is himself a trespasser; the word "title" means entitlement to ownership or tenancy of premises, and "licence" is used in the sense of leave or permission.

Anyone who is on any premises as a trespasser does not cease to be a trespasser because he has been allowed time to leave the premises.[2]

The expressions "without lawful authority or reasonable excuse" and "has with him" are discussed on pages 127 to 128.

"Weapon of offence" is defined to mean any article made or adapted for use for causing injury to or incapacitating a person, or intended by the person having it with him for such use.[3] Clearly, any gun capable of causing injury comes within this definition.

A constable[4] in uniform may arrest without warrant anyone who is, or whom he with reasonable cause suspects to be, in the act of committing the offence described.[5]

Though this offence was created primarily to deal with modern squatters who use offensive weapons to retain possession of property, those who, within the terms of the offence, trespass carrying guns in other circumstances may also be prosecuted.

Shooting on or Near the Highway

The first point to bear in mind is that the only right which the public has on a public road is to pass to and fro on it

---

[1] C.L.A. 1977 s. 12 (6).
[2] C.L.A. 1977 s. 12 (7).
[3] C.L.A. 1977 s. 8 (2).
[4] For the meaning of "constable", see note 8 on p. 94.
[5] C.L.A. 1977 s. 8 (4). For police powers of general application, see p. 85.

and to use it for other purposes reasonably necessary to that right of passage. Thus, roads are not places where anybody may shoot at will. The land on which roads are made belongs to the adjoining landowners, subject to the rights of road users and of the highway authority, or to the highway authority itself, or, in some cases, to the builder of the adjoining houses.

To this general proposition Parliament has added a number of offences dealing with shooting on or near roads. First, under the Highways Act of 1980 it is an offence, without lawful authority[1] or excuse,[2] to discharge any firearm within 50 feet[3] of the centre of a highway which consists of or comprises a carriageway as a consequence of which a user of the highway is injured, interrupted or endangered.[4]

A carriageway is defined in the Act as meaning a way constituting or comprised in a highway,[5] being a way (other than a cycle track) over which the public have a right of way for the passage of vehicles.[6] Thus, the offence will operate in the case of all public roads, and will not apply to independent footpaths and bridleways.

A highway is generally taken to be the full width of the road between its boundary hedges or ditches and this will include wide verges in some cases. Additionally, for the purposes of this offence, a highway includes bridges and tunnels where it passes over or through them.[7]

---

[1] *See* the comments on this phrase on p. 127.

[2] In order to have a lawful excuse (which is to be distinguished from "reasonable excuse" as explained on pp. 127–128) a person must show—
(a) that he honestly, but mistakenly, believed on reasonable grounds that the facts were of a certain order; and
(b) that if those facts had been of that order, his conduct would have been lawful (*Cambs. & Isle of Ely County Council and Authority v. Rust* [1972] 3 All E.R. 232). An innocent motive alone will not be enough to establish a lawful excuse (*Dickens v. Gill* (1896) 2 Q.B. 310).

[3] This is to be measured in a straight line on a horizontal plane (I.A. 1978 s. 8).

[4] H.A. 1980 s. 161 (2). The maximum punishment is a fine at level 3 on the standard scale (currently £400).

[5] *I.e.*, a public road.

[6] H.A. 1980 s. 329 (1).

[7] H.A. 1980 s. 328 (2).

Except in the Greater London Area, an offence is committed[1] by any person who in any street[2] to the obstruction, annoyance or danger of its residents or passengers wantonly discharges any firearm.[3]

In the Metropolitan Police District[4] an offence is committed[5] by any person who in any thoroughfare or public place[6] wantonly discharges any firearm to the damage or danger of any person.[7]

Shooting in Cemeteries and Burial Grounds

In certain cemeteries and burial grounds[8] it is an offence to discharge firearms except at a military funeral.[9] In the case of cemeteries provided and maintained by local authorities no such offence exists,[10] but it is made an offence wilfully[11] to create a disturbance, to commit any nuisance or

---

[1] The maximum fine on summary conviction is a fine on level 3 on the standard scale (currently £400) (C.J.A. 1967 s. 92 (1), Schedule 3, Part I). A policeman may arrest an offender without warrant if the offence is committed in his sight (T.P.C.A. 1847 s. 28).

[2] The word "street" includes any road, square, court, alley, thoroughfare or public passage (T.P.C.A. 1847 s. 3). The word does not include a place from which the public may be excluded, such as a roadway to a station or other private property (*Curtis v. Embery* (1872) L.R. 7 Exch. 369)

[3] T.P.C.A. 1847 s. 28; P.H.A. 1875 s. 171; L.G.A. 1972 s. 180, Schedule 14, paras. 23, 26.

[4] This District comprises Greater London (except the City of London and the Inner and Middle Temples) and parts of Essex, Hertfordshire and Surrey (L.G.A. 1963 s. 76 (1)).

[5] The maximum fine is at level 2 on the standard scale (currently £100) (M.P.A. 1839 s. 54). A constable belonging to the Metropolitan Police Force may arrest an offender without warrant if the offence is committed in his sight (M.P.A. 1839 s. 54).

[6] "Public place" is not defined in this context. See p. 128 for a description of places which might be considered as being within the meaning of the term.

[7] M.P.A. 1839 s. 54, para. 15.

[8] These are cemeteries and burial grounds made under the authority of an Act of Parliament which incorporates the Cemeteries Clauses Act 1847 (C.C.A. 1847 s. 1).

[9] C.C.A. 1847 ss. 3, 59. The maximum punishment is a fine at level 1 on the standard scale (currently £50).

[10] L.G.A. 1972 s. 214 (7) (8), Schedule 26, para. 14.

[11] This means deliberately and intentionally, and not by accident or inadvertence (*R. v. Senior* [1899] 1 QB 283 at pp. 290–291).

to play at any game or sport;[1] depending on circumstances, shooting may constitute one of these offences.

Possession of Firearms when Drunk

A person who is drunk[2] when in possession[3] of any loaded firearm[4] commits an offence[10] and may be arrested.[11]

---

[1] Local Authorities' Cemeteries Order 1977, Art. 18 (1). The maximum fine is at level 2 on the standard scale (currently £100) (1977 Order, Art. 19).

[2] There is no test of drunkenness in this instance, and it will be for the magistrates to decide on the evidence before them whether the accused was drunk.

[3] It is suggested that a narrower meaning for "possession" than that given on pp. 20–22 would be applicable here, i.e., that the defendant was carrying the firearm or perhaps had it within easy reach.

[4] The case of *Seamark v. Prouse and Another* [1980] 3 All E.R. 26 decided that an air rifle is a firearm for this purpose.

[10] The maximum penalties are a fine at level 1 on the standard scale (currently £50) or one month's imprisonment.

[11] L.A. 1872 s. 12. It appears that the offence is committed wherever the drunken person may be.

F

FIREARMS DEALERS

Who is a Firearms Dealer?

For the purposes of the regulations relating to firearms dealers, a firearms dealer is defined as a person who, by way of trade or business, manufactures, sells, transfers,[1] repairs, tests or proves any firearm[2] or ammunition[2] except those of the following descriptions:–

(1) An air rifle, air gun or air pistol (including their component parts and accessories[3]) not of a type declared by rules made by the Home Office[4] to be specially dangerous;

(2) Cartridges containing 5 or more shot, none of which exceeds .36 inches in diameter;

---

[1] This word is defined as including letting on hire, giving, lending and parting with possession (F.A. 1968 s. 57 (4)).

[2] As to the meaning of these words and for two general exceptions, *see* Chapter 1. There is included in the meaning of the term "firearm" any component part of it and any accessory to it designed or adapted to diminish the noise or flash caused by firing it (F.A. 1968 s. 57 (1), (4)). An imitation firearm may also be within the meaning; *see* Chapter 9.

[3] F.A. 1968 s. 57 (1).

[4] For rules so made, *see* p. 18.

(3) Ammunition for an air rifle, air gun or air pistol; and

(4) Blank cartridges not more than one inch[1] in diameter.[2]

This means that, for the purposes of the regulations later discussed in this Chapter, a person dealing in firearms is said to be a firearms dealer unless he deals **only** with one or more of the types of firearms and ammunition described above.

Registration of Firearms Dealers

The police are obliged to keep a register of firearms dealers and, with the exceptions later mentioned, to enter in it the name and places of business of any person who, having or proposing to have a place of business in the police area, applies to be registered.[3] Application should be made to the local police station on a form provided by them if you are a firearms dealer within the definition discussed above.[4] Upon registration a certificate will be issued to you.[5] A £68 fee[6] is payable.[7] The certificate lasts for three years from the date on which it was granted[8] unless the registration is cancelled under the provisions later to be considered. But

---

[1] The measurement is to be made immediately in front of the rim or cannelure of the base of the cartridge (F.A. 1968 s. 1 (4)).

[2] F.A. 1968 ss. 1 (3), (4), 57 (4).

[3] F.A. 1968 ss. 33, 57 (4). For form of register, *see* Firearms Rules 1989, Rule 10(3) and Schedule 5, Part III.

[4] F.A. 1968 s. 33 (3); Firearms Rules 1989, Rule 10(1) and Schedule 5, Part I.

[5] F.A. 1968 s. 33 (4).

[6] The amount of the fee may be varied, or abolished altogether, by order of the Home Office (F.A. 1968 s. 43 (1)).

[7] F.A. 1968 s. 35 (1), as amended by the Firearms (Variation of Fees) Order 1986. No fee is, however, payable when your only place of business was already registered in one police area and by boundary changes falls into a new police area, or when, being already registered in one police area, you propose transferring your only place of business to another police area (F.A. 1968 s. 35 (2)). If you apply to be registered for dealing at a game fair, trade fair or exhibition, agricultural show or similar event, and your principal place of business is registered for another area, the fee is £9 (F.A. 1968 s. 35 (1A)).

[8] F.A. 1968 s. 33(5); F.(A)A. 1988 s. 13 (1). Prior to amendment of s. 33(5) by the 1988 Act the certificate lasted until the 31st. May following its issue date.

in the following cases the police may, and in one case must, refuse registration:–

(*a*) Registration of the applicant **must** be refused where a Court, following conviction of the applicant, has ordered that he shall not be registered;[1]

(*b*) Registration of the applicant **may** be refused if the police are satisfied that the applicant cannot be permitted to carry on his business without danger to the public safety or to the peace;[2]

(*c*) Registration of a place of business **may** be refused if the police are satisfied that it is a place at which the applicant cannot be permitted to carry on business as a firearms dealer without danger to the public safety or to the peace.[3]

(*d*) Registration of the applicant **may** be refused unless the police are satisfied that the applicant will engage in business as a firearms dealer to a substantial extent or as an essential part of another trade, business or profession[4]

There is an appeal to the Crown Court against a refusal of the police in any of these cases.[5] Notice of the appeal must be given within 21 days from the receipt of the decision of the police to refuse.[6]

A registered firearms dealer must, on or before the expir-

---

[1] F.A. 1968 s. 34 (1). For the cases where a Court in Great Britain may make such an order, *see* pp. 146–147. Courts in Northern Ireland may also make these orders.

[2] F.A. 1968 s. 34 (2). There can, however, be no refusal on this ground where the applicant has been authorised by the Home Office to deal in prohibited weapons or prohibited ammunition, for which see pp. 11–14 (F.A. 1968 ss. 5, 34 (3), 57 (4); Transfer of Functions (Prohibited Weapons) Order 1968, Articles 2 (*a*) and 3 (1)).

For some decisions on "danger to the public safety or to the peace", although in another context, *see* p. 44.

[3] F.A. 1968 s. 34 (4). See also second part of note 2 above.

[4] F.A. 1968 ss. 34 (5), 44 (1), (2).

[5] F.A. 1968 s. 34 (1A); F.(A)A. 1988 s. 13(2)

[6] F.A. 1968 s. 44 (3) and Schedule 5, Part II. You should consult a solicitor at once if you are considering making an appeal.

ation of three years from the date of its grant, surrender his certificate of registration to the police and apply on the appropriate form for a new certificate. If granted, it will cost £36[1] and will last for a further 3-year period unless the registration is cancelled under the provisions later to be considered.[2] It can only be refused if the police are satisfied that the applicant is no longer carrying on business as a firearms dealer, or that he has ceased to have a place of business in the police area, or that he cannot be permitted to carry on such a business without danger to the public safety or to the peace.[3]

It is an offence if:–

(1) Any person, by way of trade or business, manufactures, sells, transfers,[4] tests, proves, exposes for sale or transfer,[4] or has in his possession for sale, transfer,[4] repair, test or proof, any Section 1 firearm[5], Section 1 ammunition[5] or shot gun[5] without being registered as a firearms dealer.[6]

(2) Any person makes any statement which he knows to be false for the purpose of procuring the registration of himself or another person as a firearms dealer or of procuring, whether for himself or

---

[1] The amount of the fee may be varied, or abolished altogether by order of the Home Office (F.A. 1968 s. 43 (1)).

[2] F.A. 1968 ss. 33 (5) and 35 (3), as amended by the Firearms (Variation of Fees) Order 1986; F.(A)A. 1988 s. 13(1).

[3] F.A. 1968 ss. 33 (5), 38 (1). The last ground of refusal does not apply where the dealer has been authorised by the Home Office to manufacture or deal in prohibited weapons or prohibited ammunition, as to which see pp. 11–14 (F.A. 1968 ss, 5, 38 (2); Transfer of Functions (Prohibited Weapons) Order 1968, Articles 2 (a) and 3 (1)).
For an interpretation of "danger to the public safety or to the peace", see p. 44.

[4] This word is defined as including letting on hire, giving, lending and parting with possession (F.A. 1968 s. 57 (4)).

[5] For the definition of these terms, see pp. 18–20, 20 and 41–42 respectively.

[6] F.A. 1968 s. 3 (1). The maximum punishment upon summary conviction is 6 months' imprisonment or the statutory maximum fine (currently £2000), or both; and upon indictment, 3 years' imprisonment or an unlimited fine, or both. (F.A. 1968 s. 51 (1), (2) and Schedule 6, Part I).

another person, the entry of any place of business in the register.[1]

Registration as a firearms dealer enables the dealer to do certain other things in relation to firearms and ammunition which others are not allowed to do. For example, the dealer may, within limitations, shorten the barrel of a shot gun and convert firearms and may possess, purchase and acquire[2] firearms and ammunition without holding a firearm certificate or shot gun certificate.[3]

Conditions of Registration

The police may at any time impose conditions on the registration of a person as a firearms dealer, and may, either on their own initiative or on the application of the dealer, vary or revoke any condition.[4] Where conditions are imposed on the issue of a certificate, they are to be written into it. When imposed, or varied or revoked, during the currency of a certificate, the police must give notice[5] to the dealer of the conditions or variations (giving particulars) or revocation. The notice may also require that the dealer deliver up the certificate to the police within 21 days from the date of the notice for the purpose of amending the certificate.[6] An appeal to the Crown Court lies against the imposition or variation by the police of a condition or against their refusal to vary or revoke it on the dealer's application.[7]

---

[1] F.A. 1968 s. 39 (1). The maximum punishment upon summary conviction is 6 months' imprisonment, or a fine at level 5 on the standard scale (currently £2000), or both (F.A. 1968 s. 51 (1), (2) and Schedule 6, Part I).

[2] "Acquire" means hire, accept as a gift or borrow (F.A. 1968 s. 57(4)).

[3] F.A. 1968 ss. 4 (2), (3), 8 (1). For these and other examples, see pp. 22, 37–40, 47–50.

[4] F.A. 1968 s. 36 (1).

[5] This notice may be sent by registered post or by recorded delivery service in a letter addressed to the dealer at his last or usual place of abode or at any place of business in respect of which he is registered (F.A. 1968 s. 56). It may also, of course, be delivered to him personally.

[6] F.A. 1968 s. 36 (2).

[7] F.A. 1968 ss. 36 (3) and 44. See, further, note 6 on p. 138 and the text thereto.

Failure to comply with any condition of registration is an offence,[1] and entitles the police to cancel a registration.[2]

Registration of a New Place of Business

If a person is registered as a firearms dealer in a police area and he proposes to carry on business as such a dealer at a place of business in that area which is not entered in the register kept by the police, he must notify the police of the fact and supply them with certain particulars; a form for this can be obtained from the police.[3] The police must register the new place of business unless satisfied that it is a place at which the applicant cannot be permitted to carry on business as a firearms dealer without danger to the public safety or to the peace.[4] Again, there is a right of appeal to the Crown Court against any police refusal to register.[5]

A registered firearms dealer[6] commits an offence if he has a place of business which is not entered in the register for the police area in which the place of business is situated and carries on business as a firearms dealer at that place.[7]

Removal from Register of Dealer's Name or Place of Business by the Police

The name of a firearms dealer or his place of business is removable from the police register in the following circumstances:–

---

[1] F.A. 1968 s. 39 (3). The maximum punishment upon summary conviction is 6 months' imprisonment, or a fine at level 5 on the standard scale (currently £2000), or both (F.A. 1968 s. 51 (1) and Schedule 6, Part I).

[2] F.A. 1968 s. 38 (3). *See also*, item (2) on p. 142.

[3] F.A. 1968 ss. 37 (1), 57 (4). Firearms Rules 1989, Rule 10(2) and Schedule 5, Part II.

[4] F.A. 1968 s. 37 (1), (2). For an interpretation of "danger to the public safety or to the peace", *see* p. 44.

[5] F.A. 1968 ss. 37 (3) and 44. See, further, note 6 on p. 138 and the text thereto.

[6] A registered firearms dealer is defined as one who is either, as described above, registered in Great Britain or is registered in Northern Ireland under the Firearms Act 1920 s. 8 or any enactment of the Parliament of Northern Ireland amending or substituted for that section (F.A. 1968 s. 57 (4)).

[7] F.A. 1968 s. 39 (2). The maximum punishment upon summary conviction is 6 months' imprisonment, or a fine at level 5 on the standard scale (currently £2000), or both (F.A. 1968 s. 51 (1) and Schedule 6, Part I).

(1) The police **shall** remove the dealer's name if, after giving reasonable notice[1] to the dealer, they are satisfied that:–

   (*a*) He is no longer carrying on business as a firearms dealer; or

   (*b*) He has has ceased to have a place of business in the police area; or

   (*c*) He cannot be permitted to continue to carry on business as a firearms dealer without danger to the public safety or to the peace.[2]

(2) The police **may**, if satisfied that a dealer has failed to comply with any of the conditions of registration[3] which have been imposed, remove from the register the dealer's name or any place of business of his to which the condition relates.[4]

(3) The police **may** remove a dealer's place of business from the register if satisfied that it is one at which the dealer cannot be permitted to carry on business as such without danger to the public safety or to the peace.[5]

(4) The police **shall** remove a dealer's name from the register if the dealer so desires.[6]

(5) The police **shall** remove the dealer's name from the register if:–

   (*a*) the dealer fails, on or before its expiration, to surrender his certificate of registration to the police or to apply for a new certificate; **and**

---

[1] As to service of the notice, *see* note 5 on p. 140.

[2] F.A. 1968 s. 38 (1). There can, however, be no refusal under para. (*c*) where the dealer has been authorised by the Home Office to deal in prohibited weapons or ammunition, as to which, *see* Chapter 2 (F.A. 1968 ss. 5, 38 (2); Transfer of Functions (Prohibited Weapons) Order 1968, Articles 2 (*a*) and 3 (1)).

For some decisions on "danger to the public safety or to the peace", although in another context, see p. 44.

[3] As to these conditions, *see* pp. 140–141.

[4] F.A. 1968 s. 38 (3).

[5] F.A. 1968 s. 38 (4). See also second part of note 2 above.

[6] F.A. 1968 s. 38 (5).

(*b*) the police give written notice[1] to the dealer requiring him to do whatever he has failed to do under paragraph (*a*) above; **and**

(*c*) the dealer fails to comply with the written notice within 21 days from its date or such further time as the police may in special circumstances allow.[2]

Again, there is a right of appeal to the Crown Court in any of these cases.[3]

On removal of a dealer's name (but not his place of business) from the register, the police will require the dealer by written notice[1] to surrender his certificate of registration. Failure to do so within 21 days from the date of the notice is an offence.[4] If an appeal is made against the removal of the dealer's name from the register and is not successful, the period of 21 days will, instead, run from the date on which the appeal was abandoned or dismissed.[5]

The Register of Firearms Transactions

Every person who by way of trade or business manufactures, sells or transfers[6] firearms[7] or ammunition[7] must provide and keep a register of transactions[8] and must enter,

---

[1] As to service of the notice, *see* note 5 on p. 140.

[2] F.A. 1968 s. 38 (6).

[3] F.A. 1968 ss. 38 (7) and 44. *See* further, note 6 on p. 138 and the text thereto.

[4] F.A. 1968 s. 38 (8); F.(A(A. 1988 s. 13(3). The maximum punishment upon summary conviction is a fine at level 3 on the standard scale (currently £400) (F.A. 1968 s. 51 (1) and Schedule 6, Part I).

[5] F.A. 1968 s. 38 (8) proviso.

[6] This word is defined as including letting on hire, giving, lending and parting with possession (F.A. 1968 s. 57 (4)).

[7] As to the meaning of these words and for two general exceptions, *see* Chapter 1.

[8] For form of register and directions for keeping it, *see* Firearms Rules 1989, Rule 10(4) and Schedule 5, Part IV.

or cause to be entered, in it certain prescribed particulars.[1]

In the following cases, however, this requirement need not be complied with:–

(1) When the firearms are air weapons[2] or component parts of, or accessories to, air weapons;[3]

(2) When the ammunition is any of the types described in items (2), (3) and (4) on pages 136 and 137 of this Chapter;[3]

(3) When firearms or ammunition are sold by auction in accordance with the terms of a police permit issued to the auctioneer.[4]

The rules about keeping a register may be relaxed in the following situation. If it appears to the police that:–

(a) a person required to be registered as a firearms dealer[5] carries on a trade or business in the course of which he manufactures, tests or repairs component parts or accessories for shot guns,[6] but not complete shot guns; **and**

(b) it is impossible to assemble a shot gun[6] from the parts likely to come into that person's possession in the course of that trade or business;

the police may, if they think fit, by written notice[7] given

---

[1] F.A. 1968 s. 40 (1). Failure to do so constitutes an offence, the maximum punishment for which on summary conviction is 6 months' imprisonment, or a fine at level 5 on the standard scale (currently £2000), or both (F.A. 1968 ss 40 (5), 51 (1), (2) and Schedule 6, Part I). The prescribed particulars, as amended by the Firearms Rules 1989, Rule 10(5), are reproduced in Appendix I at the end of the book. They may be further amended from time to time by rules made by the Home Office (F.A. 1968 ss. 40 (7), 53 and Schedule 4).

[2] An air weapon is defined as an air rifle, air gun or air pistol not of a type declared by rules made by the Home Office (for which *see* p. 18) to be specially dangerous (F.A. 1968 ss. 1 (3)(b), 57 (4)).

[3] F.A. 1968 s. 40 (2).

[4] F.A. 1968 ss. 9 (2), 40 (6). For such permits, see pp. 52–54.

[5] As to the persons required to be so registered, *see* pp. 136–137.

[6] For the definition of "shot gun", see pp. 41–42.

[7] As to the service of the notice, *see* note 5 on p. 140.

to that person exempt his transactions in those parts and accessories from all or any of the requirements for keeping a register. This exemption lasts "so long as the notice is in force".[1]

Every entry required to be made in the register must be made within 24 hours after the transaction to which it relates. In the case of a sale or transfer[2] of firearms or ammunition, the dealer[3] must, at the time, require the purchaser or transferee, if not known to him, to furnish particulars sufficient for identification[4] and must immediately enter those particulars in the register.[5]

A person keeping a register shall, unless required to surrender it to the police,[6] keep it for such a period so that each entry shall be available for inspection for at least five years from the date of the entry.[7]

A person keeping a register of firearms transactions must, if asked to do so by a constable[8] authorised in writing to make the demand by the chief officer of police, allow the constable to enter his premises to inspect all stock in hand. The register must be produced for inspection to any constable authorised in the same way and to any officer of customs and excise.[9] If asked to do so, the constable must produce his written authority.[10]

---

[1] F.A. 1968 s. 41. It is not clear whether the notice should be given for a limited or unlimited time; if given for an unlimited time, it may presumably be cancelled by the police at any subsequent time by a further notice served in the same way as the original notice.

[2] This word is defined as including let on hire, give, lend and part with possession (F.A. 1968 s. 57 (4)).

[3] Or his employee, or other person on his behalf (F.A. 1968 s. 40 (1), (3)).

[4] It is suggested that the full names and address of the person concerned will be sufficient.

[5] F.A. 1968 s. 40 (3). Failure to comply with any requirement in this paragraph is an offence (F.A. 1968 s. 40 (5)). For the maximum punishments, see note 1 on p. 144.

[6] As to which, see p. 143.

[7] F.A. 1968 s. 40(3A); F.(A)A 1988 s. 13(4). This requirement applies only to entries made after the coming into force of s. 13(4) of the 1988 Act which occurred on 1st February 1989.

[8] For the meaning of "constable", see note 8 on p. 144.

[9] Failure to do so is an offence (F.A. 1968 s. 40(5)). For the maximum punishments, see note 1 on p. 144.

[10] F.A. 1968 s. 40 (4); F.(A)A. 1988 s. 23(3).

It is an offence if a person knowingly makes any false entry in a register of firearms transactions.[1]

As we have seen,[2] a person may buy from a registered firearms dealer a firearm for export without holding a firearm or shot gun certificate. When this happens, the dealer must within 48 hours of the sale send[3] a notice of it to the chief officer of police in whose register the dealer's premises are entered.[4] The notice must contain the same particulars of the transaction as the dealer is required to enter in his register for other kinds of transaction.[5] The notice, and the particulars to be entered in the register, shall also include the number and place of issue of any passport held by the buyer of the firearm.[6]

Consequences of Conviction of Firearms Dealers

When a registered firearms dealer[7] is convicted of almost any offence[8] connected with firearms or ammunition, the convicting court has power to order as follows:–

(1) That the name of the dealer be removed from the register; and

---

[1] F.A. 1968 s. 40 (5). For punishments, *see* note 1 on p. 144.

[2] Item (16) on p. 27.

[3] The notice is to be sent by registered post or recorded delivery service.

[4] F.(A)A. 1988 s. 18(2). Failure to comply is an offence with a maximum punishment on summary conviction of 6 months' imprisonment, or a fine at level 5 on the standard scale (currently £2000), or both (F.(A)A. 1988 s. 18(5)).

[5] For those particulars, see note 1 on p. 144.

[6] F.(A)A. 1988 s. 18(3)(4).

[7] For the definition of "registered firearms dealer", *see* note 6 on p. 141.

[8] More precisely, the offences are: (i) offences against the enactments relating to customs or excise in respect of the import or export of any firearms or ammunition, except any of the types described in items (1) to (4) on pp. 136–137; (ii) all offences under the Firearms Act 1968 except (briefly):–

(a) Obtaining or possessing a shot gun without a shot gun certificate and failing to comply with a condition of such a certificate (F.A. 1968 s. 2).

(b) Person under 15 handling a shot gun without an adult's supervision or whilst not covered with a gun cover (F.A. 1968 s. 22 (3)).

(c) Giving a shot gun or ammunition for a shot gun to a person under 15 (F.A. 1968 s. 24 (3)).

(d) An offence relating specifically to air weapons (F.A. 1968 s. 45 (2)).

References above to a shot gun include references to component parts of a shot gun and to any accessories for diminishing its noise or flash (F.A. 1968 ss. 45(2), 57(4)).

(2) That neither the dealer nor any person who acquires his business, nor any person who took part in the management of the business and was knowingly a party to the offence, shall be registered as a firearms dealer; and

(3) That any person who, after the date of the court's order, knowingly employs in the management of his business the dealer convicted of the offence, or any person who was knowingly a party to the offence, shall not be registered as a firearms dealer or, if so registered, shall be liable to be removed from the register;[1] and

(4) That any stock-in-hand of the business shall be disposed of by sale or otherwise in accordance with such directions as may be contained in the order.[2]

A dealer against whom such an order is made may appeal against it in the same way as he may appeal against his conviction, and the court may, if it thinks fit, suspend the operation of the order pending the appeal.[3]

---

[1] The evident purpose of an order that a person shall be "liable to be removed from the register" is to enable a court subsequently, after proof of a conviction under item (3) of the text, to remove from the register an employer of the convicted persons.

[2] F.A. 1968 s. 45 (1), (2).

[3] F.A. 1968 s. 45 (3). As to an appeal, *see*, further, note 6 on p. 138 and the text thereto.

APPENDICES

APPENDIX A

ANTIQUE FIREARMS: HOME OFFICE GUIDANCE TO THE POLICE[1]

Table to be used as a guide in considering whether a firearm is to be
regarded as an antique

Antiques

(a) All muzzle-loading firearms
(b) Breech-loading firearms capable of discharging a rim-fire cartridge exceeding .23 inches calibre (or its metric equivalent), but not 9 mm.
(c) Breech-loading firearms using ignition systems other than rim-fire or centre-fire. (These include pin-fire and needle-fire ignition systems.).

Not antiques

(a) Breech-loading firearms capable of discharging either:
   (i) a centre-fire cartridge; or
   (ii) a rim-fire cartridge not exceeding .23 inches calibre (or its metric equivalent); or
   (iii) a 9 mm. rim-fire cartridge.
(b) Ammunition. (See note (i) below).
(c) Firearms of modern manufacture. (See note (ii) below).

Note (1): The exemption does not apply to ammunition, and the possession of ammunition suitable for use with an otherwise antique firearm will normally indicate that the firearm is not possessed as a curio or ornament.

Note (ii): The exemption does not apply to firearms of modern manufacture which otherwise conform to the description above. Thus modern firing replicas of muzle-loading firearms will require to be held on certificate. "Modern manufacture" should be taken to mean "manufactured since (or during) the Second World War".

---

[1] *"Firearms Law: Guidance to the Police"* (1989). This guidance adds that many cases, however, will depend on their own facts and each will need to be assessed on its merits. For further references to antique firearms, see pp. 9–10.

G

APPENDIX B

MUSEUMS FOR WHICH FIREARMS LICENCES MAY BE ISSUED[1]

The Armouries, H.M. Tower of London
The National Army Museum
The National Museum of Wales
The Royal Air Force Museum
The Science Museum
The Victoria and Albert Museum
The Royal Marines Museum
The Fleet Air Arm Museum
The Royal Navy Museum
The Royal Navy Submarine Museum
The British Museum
The Imperial War Museum
The National Maritime Museum
The National Museums of Scotland
The National Museums and Galleries on Merseyside
The Wallace Collection
Any other museum or similar institution in Great Britain[2] which has as its purpose, or one of its purposes, the preservation for the public benefit of a collection of historical, artistic or scientific interest which includes or is to include firearms and which is maintained wholly or mainly[3] out of money provided by Parliament or by a local authority.

---

[1] F.(A)A. 1988 s. 19 & Sch., paras. 1(1), 5. For further references to these licences, see pp. 58–61.

[2] For the meaning of "Great Britain", see note 7 on p. 27.

[3] The word "mainly" probably means "more than half". (*Fawcett Properties Ltd. v. Bucks C.C.* [1960] 3 All E.R. 503 at 512, H.L.).

APPENDIX C

CLOSE SEASONS FOR SHOOTING GAME AND DEER[1]

Section 1[2]

Black game	11th December to 19th August, except in Somerset, Devon and that part of the New Forest which lies in Hampshire where it is 11th December to 31st August.
Bustard or wild turkey	2nd March to 31st August.
Grouse or red game	11th December to 11th August.
Partridge	2nd February to 31st August.
Pheasant	2nd February to 30th September.

Section 2

Hare	None.[3]

---

[1] In the case of all the birds and animals in Sections 1 and 2 shooting on Sunday and Christmas Day is forbidden (G.A. 1831 s. 3).

All dates are inclusive.

The close seasons are not operative in cases where the Ministry of Agriculture impose a requirement that game be killed to prevent damage to crops, pasture, foodstuffs, livestock, trees, hedges, banks or any works on land (A.A. 1947 s. 98 (1), (2)).

For close seasons for the purposes of the Wildlife and Countryside Act 1981, see Appendix E (2).

[2] G.A. 1831 s. 3.

[3] According to *Oke's Game Laws*, 5th Edition, p. 8. the period is 1st March to 31st July. This book does not, however, indicate whether or not the dates are inclusive, nor quote any statutory authority for the period. On the other hand, *Oke* at p. 118 takes the view, supported by *Halsbury's Laws of England*, 4th Edition, Vol. 2, para. 288, that there is no specified close season for hares; and this is thought to be the better view. Certainly, there is no period of the year during which it is an offence to kill hares, except for the restrictions on the rights of occupiers to shoot hares and rabbits on certain moorlands and unenclosed lands at certain times of the year, for which *see* pp. 114–115.

Section 3[1]

Male red deer, fallow deer and sika deer	1st May to 31st July.
Female red deer, fallow deer, roe deer and sika deer	1st March to 31st October.
Male roe deer	1st November to 31st March.

---

[1] D.A. 1963 s. 1 (1) and Sch. 1; R.D.A. 1977 ss. 1, 2 (2). Further species of deer, with close seasons for them, may be added by order of the Home Office (D.A. 1963 s. 1 (2)). For instances where deer may be shot out of season, *see* pp. 96–97.

APPENDIX D

WILD BIRDS WHICH ARE PROTECTED BY SPECIAL PENALTIES[1]

Avocet
Bee-eater
Bittern
Bittern, Little
Bluethroat
Brambling
Bunting, Cirl
Bunting, Lapland
Bunting, Snow
Buzzard, Honey
Chough
Corncrake
Crake, Spotted
Crossbills (all species)
Curlew, Stone
Divers (all species)
Dotterel
Duck, Long-tailed
Eagle, Golden
Falcon, Gyr
Fieldfare
Firecrest
Garganey
Godwit, Black-tailed
[2]Goldeneye
[2]Goose, Greylag (in Outer
  Hebrides, Caithness,
  Sutherland and Wester
  Ross only)
Goshawk
Grebe, Black-necked
Grebe, Slavonian
Greenshank

Gull, Little
Gull, Mediterranean
Harriers (all species)
Heron, Purple
Hobby
Hoopoe
Kingfisher
Kite, Red
Merlin
Oriole, Golden
Osprey
Owl, Barn
Owl, Snowy
Peregrine
Petrel, Leach's
Phalarope, Red-necked
[2]Pintail
Plover, Kentish
Plover, Little-Ringed
Quail, Common
Redstart, Black
Redwing
Rosefinch, Scarlet
Ruff
Sandpiper, Green
Sandpiper, Purple
Sandpiper, Wood
Scaup
Scoter, Common
Scoter, Velvet
Serin
Shorelark
Shrike, Red-backed

---

[1] W.C.A. 1981 Schedule 1. For references to this list of birds, see pp. 90–91.
[2] The special penalties only apply to these birds during their close seasons, for which see Appendix E, Part (2).

155

Spoonbill
Stilt, Black-winged
Stint, Temminck's
Swan, Bewick's
Swan, Hooper
Tern, Black
Tern, Little
Tern, Roseate
Tit, Bearded

Tit, Crested
Treecreeper, Short-toed
Warbler, Cetti's
Warbler, Dartford
Warbler, Marsh
Warbler, Savi's
Whimbrel
Woodlark
Wryneck

APPENDIX E

(1) WILD BIRDS WHICH MAY BE KILLED OR TAKEN OUTSIDE THE CLOSE SEASON[1]

Capercaillie
Coot
Duck, Tufted
Gadwall
Goldeneye
Goose, Canada
Goose, Greylag
Goose, Pink-footed
Goose, White-fronted[2]
Mallard

Moorhen
Pintail
Plover, Golden
Pochard
Shoveler
Snipe, Common
Teal
Wigeon
Woodcock

(2) CLOSE SEASONS OUTSIDE WHICH WILD BIRDS LISTED AT (1) ABOVE MAY BE KILLED, INJURED OR TAKEN[3]

Capercaillie and woodcock[4] .... 1st February to 30th September.
Snipe .... 1st February to 11th August.
Wild duck and wild geese in or over any area below high water mark of ordinary spring tides .... 21st February to 31st August.
In any other case .... 1st February to 31st August.

---

[1] W.C.A. 1981 s. 2 (1) (3), Schedule 2, Part I. For some exceptions, see p. 88, item (1).
See Part (2) of this Appendix for details of close seasons.
[2] In England and Wales only.
[3] W.C.A. 1981 s. 2 (4). All dates are inclusive. *See* p. 88 for further details.
These close seasons may be varied, and special protection for additional periods given, by Government order (W.C.A. 1981 s. 2 (5) (6)).
[4] This period does not apply to woodcock in Scotland which therefore in that country fall under the heading "In any other case".

APPENDIX F

WILD BIRDS WHICH MAY BE KILLED, INJURED OR TAKEN AT ANY TIME[1] BY AUTHORISED PERSONS[2]

Crow
Dove, collared
Gull, Great Black-backed
Gull, Lesser Black-backed
Gull, Herring
Jackdaw
Jay
Magpie
Pigeon, Feral[3]
Rook
Sparrow, House
Starling
Woodpigeon

---

[1] Except in Scotland on Sundays and Christmas Days.
[2] W.C.A. 1981 s. 2 (2) (3), Schedule 2, Part II. *See* pp. 88–89 for further details.
[3] *I.e.* gone wild.

APPENDIX G

LICENCES FOR SHOOTING WILD BIRDS[1] AND WILD ANIMALS[2]

Purpose for which licence may be granted	*Type of wildlife to which it is applicable*	*Issuing Authority*
1. Scientific or educational	Both	The Nature Conservancy Council[3] or the appropriate Secretary of State[4] for birds;[5] the Council in other cases
2. Conserving wild birds or wild animals	Both	
3. Protecting a collection of wild birds or a zoological collection	Both	The appropriate Secretary of State[4] for birds. The Council for wild animals

---

[1] In this context game birds are included. For their definition and that for wild birds, see p. 87. (W.C.A. 1981 ss. 16 (1), 27 (1)).

[2] W.C.A. 1981 ss. 16 (1)–(3) (9), 27 (1). Licences may be: general or specific; granted to persons of a class or to a particular person; subject to compliance with specified conditions; modified or revoked at any time by the issuing authority. A licence will be valid for the period (not exceeding two years) stated in it (if not previously modified or revoked), and a reasonable charge may be made for it (W.C.A. 1981 s. 16 (5) (6) (b)).

[3] The Council's address is 19–20 Belgrave Square, London SW1X 8PY.

[4] I.e.: (1) in England, the Secretary of State for the Department of the Environment and, in Wales, the Secretary of State for Wales; in both countries applications should be made to the Department at Tollgate House, Houlton Street, Bristol BS2 9DJ; (2) in Scotland, the Secretary of State for Scotland, with applications to be made to the Scottish Home and Health Department, St. Andrews House, Edinburgh EH1 3DE.

[5] The Department of the Environment advises that, in the case of licences which concern birds and where there is an alternative issuing authority, applicants should contact the Nature Conservancy Council in the first instance.

Purpose for which licence may be granted	Type of wildlife to which it is applicable	Issuing Authority
4. Preserving public health or public safety and (for birds) air safety	Both	The Ministry of Agriculture or the appropriate Secretary of State[1]
5. Taxidermy	Wild birds	The appropriate Secretary of State[2]
6. Preventing the spread of disease	Both	
7. Preventing serious damage to livestock,[3] foodstuffs for livestock,[3] crops, vegetables, fruit, growing timber or any other form of property or to fisheries	Both	The Ministry of Agriculture or the appropriate Secretary of State[2]
8. Providing food for human consumption. Licences restricted to— (a) gannets on the Island of Sula Sgeir, (b) gulls' eggs (c) lapwings' eggs at any time before 15th April in any year	Wild birds	The appropriate Secretary of State[2]

---

[1] Applications should be submitted as follows: in England, to the local Divisional Office of the Ministry of Agriculture; in Wales, to the Welsh Office, Crown Building, Cathays Park, Cardiff CF1 3NQ; in Scotland, to the Department of Agriculture and Fisheries for Scotland, Chesser House, 500 Gorgie Road, Edinburgh EH11 3AW.

[2] I.e.: (1) in England, the Secretary of State for the Department of the Environment and, in Wales, the Secretary of State for Wales; in both countries applications should be made to the Department at Tollgate House, Houlton Street, Bristol BS2 9DJ; (2) in Scotland, the Secretary of State for Scotland, with applications to be made to the Scottish Home and Health Department, St. Andrews House, Edinburgh EH1 3DE.

[3] For the definition of "livestock", see note 6 on p. 90.

APPENDIX H

WILD ANIMALS WHICH MAY NOT BE KILLED OR TAKEN BY CERTAIN METHODS[1]

Badger
Bats, Horseshoe (all species)
Bats, Typical (all species)
Cat, Wild
Dolphin, Bottle-nosed
Dolphin, Common
Dormice (all species)
Hedgehog
Marten, Pine
Otter, Common
Polecat
Porpoise, Harbour (otherwise known as Common porpoise)
Shrews (all species)
Squirrel, Red

---

[1] W.C.A. 1981 Schedule 6. For references to this list of animals, see pp. 92–94.

APPENDIX I

PARTICULARS TO BE ENTERED BY FIREARMS DEALER IN REGISTER OF TRANSACTIONS

1. The quantities and description of firearms and ammunition manufactured and the dates thereof.

2. The quantities and description of firearms and ammunition purchased or acquired with the names and addresses of the sellers or transferors and the dates of the several transactions.

3. The quantities and description of firearms and ammunition accepted for sale, repair, test, proof, cleaning, storage, destruction or other purpose, with the names and addresses of the transferors and the dates of the several transactions.

4. The quantities and descriptions of firearms and ammunition sold or transferred with the names and addresses of the purchasers or transferees and (except in cases where the purchaser or transferee is a registered dealer) the areas in which the firearm certificates were issued, and the dates of the several transactions.

5. The quantities and description of firearms and ammunition in possession for sale or transfer at the date of the last stocktaking or such other date in each year as may be specified in the register.[1]

6. In the case of a firearm sold for export to a buyer without a firearm or shot gun certificate, the number and place of issue of any passport held by the buyer.[2]

---

[1] F.A. 1968, Sch. 4; Firearms Rules 1989 Rule 10(5). *See* pp. 143–146 for further details and references to definitions of the words "transfers", "firearms" and "ammunition". The words "transferees" and "transferors" are to be construed according to the definition of "transfers". The word "acquire" means hire, accept as a gift or borrow (F.A. 1968 s. 57 (4)).

[2] F.(A)A. 1988 s. 18(4).

Index

INDEX

[165]

Q

R

S